2011

D1552708

# A Few Good Golf Stories

**Joe Black**

Copyright © 2011 Joe Black

All photographs are taken from Joe Black's personal collection.

Most of my stories are events I was personally involved with or answer questions raised by friends over the years. I have been telling the stories for over fifty years. The events are as I remember them. If I offend anyone I am truly sorry.

All rights reserved. No part of this book may be reproduced in any form or by any electronic or mechanical means, including information storage and retrieval systems, without written permission from the publisher, except for a reviewer who may quote passages in a review.

ISBN 978-0-9819023-2-6

Austin Brothers
Publishing

Published by Austin Brothers Publishing

www.austinbrotherspublishing.com

*I dedicate this book to my wife, Susan. Without her it would not have been written. She provided all of the typing, the emailing and the encouragement necessary to keep me going and I love her for it. She truly is my soul mate.*

## Acknowledgments:

Special thanks to: Claude Dollins of The Dollins Group for help and support during this project - it is deeply appreciated. To Hardin-Simmons University, and Dennis Harp, Vice President, for your encouragement and support. To Brian Elliott of Nike Golf whose breakfast conversation got it all started. And to Terry Austin for all you did to resurrect the project.

# The Stories

# *Forward.*

I have known Joe Black since our college days at Hardin-Simmons University. We have kept in touch over the years and he has told me some of his stories from time to time. His book will be like sitting down for a glass of wine with an old friend.

### Doyle "Texas Dolly" Brunson

Joe Black has devoted his adult lifetime to golf and has contributed to the great game in many ways, most prominently as President of the PGA of America in 1981-1982. But most of my experience and contact with him came over the seven years he worked as a rules official and supervisor on the PGA Tour.

Unlike most of the other major sports, rules officials in golf are behind-the-scenes people most of the time. But they are no less vital to the successful playing of professional tournaments than are the umpires in baseball and the on-field officials in football. Joe Black was certainly one of the best in my years on the Tour, a man of integrity and full knowledge of the complicated and voluminous Rules of Golf.

A lot happened on the Tour during his seven seasons and he has brought to life his recollections of those years and his many years in other roles in this interesting book that adds another literary touch to the history of golf. I know that it will bring many memories to all who have followed the game and enlighten those who weren't around at the time.

### Arnold Palmer

I thought I'd write a few words about my old friend Joe Black. It is easy to say that he has been a great friend to golf, and he has, but his devotion to the game has come into form in so many capacities.

*Joe started caddying at the age of ten. The "golf bug" must have hit him early because he saw that he wanted to make his living in golf rather than chopping and picking cotton or working in a grocery store in the west Texas town of Lamesa. He became a fine player at Hardin-Simmons University where he played on the 1953 NAIA Championship Team. After leaving Hardin-Simmons he played the PGA Tour for two years. He must have made a lot of friends during this period because a number of players saw to it that Joe was selected to run the organization that was the predecessor today's PGA Tour. After seven years running the Tour, Joe took the head professional job a Brookhaven Country Club in Dallas. His influence and reputation grew so much that during his tenure as president of the PGA of American in 1981-1982 he was instrumental in the negotiations regarding the importance of the relationship between the two professional organizations – the players and the club professionals – for the collective good of the game. The mutual respect lives today, and it is vital in order for the game to stay healthy and strong.*

*The Joe Black Cup Matches is a 30 year competition between the Northern and Southern sections of the PGA. One can only imagine the rivalry and keenness this event creates. Apart from his other duties and travels, Joe and his good friend Verde Dickey founded Western Golf Properties. After that successful stint in Scottsdale, Arizona, Joe has returned to Texas and lives in Bee Cave where he has spent considerable time helping Austin's First Tee organization and other charitable endeavors.*

*Joe has always been a leader in the game and a voice of reason and authority. His reputation and integrity, coupled with his love for the game, commands our respect and profound thanks.*

**Ben Crenshaw**

*Fifty years ago I met Joe Black at a back yard cook out in Dallas, Texas. Neither of us could have imagined the casual meeting would be the beginning of a lifelong friendship.*

*Over time, we found that we shared numerous beliefs like a work ethic that allows for no entitlement and rewards only that which you earn. We agreed then and now that goals must be attained and success must be earned by hard work and dedication.*

*The following pages will recount the accomplishments and honors Joe earned in various areas of the sporting world. His special commitment to golf has become legendary and Joe has earned the respect of honorable men and women where ever golf is played.*

*Joe's dedication to the sport of golf is evidenced not only by those who have put their trust in him, but by his impressive history within the sport. From the Presidency of the PGA of America, to his Chairmanship of the Ryder Cup Matches, to his astounding record of forty-eight years as a trusted Rules Official at the Master's Tournament, Joe's accomplishments have helped shape the sport.*

*It has been my privilege to know Joe Black as a co-worker, a business partner, a golf instructor and the dearest of friends. There is no finer man.*

*Now, let's enjoy a carefully selected and prepared group of golf stories by a man who was there.*

**Verde Dickey**


*My fifteen years on The Tour were mostly under the supervision of Joe Black our Golf commissioner. If anybody can tell stories about the PGA Tour, Joe Black can. I can't wait to read them.*

**Jack Burke**


*I know all of you will enjoy this book of stories from Joe Black. Joe has never failed to come up with a really good story and he tells them so well. We have been friends since we first met when he was the new lead professional at Brookhaven in Dallas. We later worked together as the presidents of the two Texas sections of the PGA. Joe went on to be the national president of the association receiving the PGA's highest awards.*

*I have always found Joe to be the consummate professional in whatever he does. He has always been a mover and shaker and ready to take on a new challenge any time one is presented. Having participated as a Rules Official at The Masters and many of the other major PGA tournaments as well as the Ryder Cup you can imagine how many great stories he has to tell.*

*I know you will find this book to be interesting and a joy to read.*

**George Hannon**

# *Introduction*

"Each story has a beginning and an end. Everything in between is in the eyes of the teller, so start writing."

These remarks were made by Red Steagall, Cowboy Poet of Texas, during a concert in Alpine, Texas, at the Cowboy Poetry Gathering at Sul Ross State University encouraging everyone to write their family history.

For years, I have been sharing my stories regarding:

- The Tour
- PGA of America
- Friendship with the tour's elite players
- Brookhaven Country Club
- Club Corporation of America
- Rules of Golf

Every time I tell these stories I am told I should write a book. "A Few Good Golf Stories" is a collection of stories from different aspects of my life in golf. Some will be historical in nature but have never been recorded. Some were well known but have been lost over time. I am hopeful you will find these stories interesting and entertaining.

After several months at the computer I can tell you, writing, publishing, and marketing a book is more difficult than shooting 33 on the back nine at Augusta.

Thank you in advance for your support. It means so much to me to share this part of my life and the impact the game of golf has had on all of our lives.

**Joe Black**

# Humble Beginnings

I was born in Snyder, Texas, August 8, 1933. My parents were Joel and Bonnie Black and I was the third of six children. I have two older brothers, Norman and Marvin, two younger brothers, Isaiah and Daulton, and a sister, Nancy. We moved to Lamesa when I was one year old and lived there off and on until I graduated from high school. I was what was known as a "depression baby," and grew up in the Great Depression. We were probably more fortunate than many because my father at least had a job for a good part of the depression. He worked as a laborer in a cottonseed meal plant where cottonseed was processed into cubes to feed livestock.

The first real memory I have growing up as a child is living on South 7th Street in Lamesa. This was the very last street on the south side of town. We lived in a small two-bedroom house with no indoor plumbing and a screened in porch on the back of the house. We had an outhouse in back. Because of the makeup of our family, all of the boys slept on the back porch summer and winter.

It could get unbearably hot in the summertime and unbelievably cold in the winter time. The summertime wasn't as bad as the winter because the wind always blew in Lamesa. At least the wind blowing in the summer helped make it a little more bearable to sleep at night. When that cold north wind blew in the winter, we piled all the quilts and blankets we could find on the bed just to stay warm.

The first few years, we only had one bed on the back porch so we all slept together. Of course, going to the bathroom at night was a real adventure, particularly in the winter. When you climbed back in bed, you knew that you were going to get a punch from the brother you were sleeping next too.

You were either going to get him very cold or very wet or both.

My early childhood was like most children growing up in a large family in the depression. There was not much in the way of toys or other things to play with so we had to create our own games and ways to interact with each other. We lived on the edge of town with a large pasture behind us that became a playground. There were major war games played, as well as the traditional Cowboys and Indians. Of course, the big foray from time to time was looking for snakes and other wildlife that we could capture and keep as pets. All of my brothers and I were pretty compatible so we did not have too many fights or other disagreements. I think living in a large family tends to create more compatibility.

Lamesa was the county seat of Dawson County with a population of 10,000 people. It was by far the largest community in the county. Lamesa is from a Spanish term meaning "tabletop," and as the name implies Dawson County was just like a tabletop. It is in the center of the cotton growing part of Texas. The land was so flat you could see for miles without an obstructed view, but all you could see was cotton fields. At the time, it was all dry land cotton farming. The aquifer under that part of Texas had not been discovered, so there was no irrigation.

When I was growing up in Lamesa, it was known as the dust bowl days. There was a severe drought for seven years in West Texas. Because there was no irrigation and because the cotton fields were plowed every fall after the cotton was gathered, there was no plant material to hold the soil in place. With windy conditions we had sandstorms that could last for days. When a sandstorm developed, the sky would turn black. There were days when you could look out the window and could not see the house across the street even though it had its lights on. After a sandstorm, the house would have as much as a quarter of an inch of sand on all of the furniture in the house. During the sandstorm, you could see the sand filtering through the house. During a bad sandstorm, the paint of an automobile could be sandblasted off.

You could tell when the farmers got enough rain to make a crop because they would all buy a new pickup truck. They would also pay off their notes at the bank and their accounts at the grocery store. The banks, grocery stores, and other merchants in town essentially financed the cotton farming industry.

When I was growing up it was common that everyone in the family had to help support the family financially. Both my father and mother came from families with eight children. They also came from families who were ranchers. Most families have a lot of children because the children provided the workforce for the ranchers or farmers. From a very early age, everyone had chores to do to help make the ranches function.

It was no different in our family even though we lived in town; everyone in the family had to work to make enough money. From an early age, dad would contract out the kids to farmers to hoe the weeds in the cotton fields in the summertime to keep the weeds from competing with the cotton for fertilizer and water. When the cotton was ready to be picked our father would contract with farmers for us to help pick the cotton. As a matter of fact, during cotton picking time, the schools would close so that all the kids could be available to pick cotton. At the end of each week during these times, my dad would collect the money we earned and it would be used to pay family expenses. Usually on Saturday, my dad would give us enough money to go to the movie and buy popcorn and a drink.

When I was about 10 years old, someone told me that I could make fifty cents a round as a caddie at Lamesa Country Club, and if I did a good job I may get a ten cent tip. This sounded like a pretty good deal to me. It was as much money as I made chopping and picking cotton or helping my dad who had become a carpenter. When he built a house, he would have us dig ditches for the water and sewer lines and mix and pour the concrete for the slab. We would also help with the framing of the house, installing sheetrock, putting up rafters, and the roofing. It seemed to me that being a caddie would be a lot easier work than helping build houses or working in the cotton fields.

I made a deal with my dad that if he would let me caddie instead of working with him that I would give him the money I made to help with the family expenses. He finally agreed. That is how I entered the golf business.

Lamesa Country Club was a nine hole sand green golf course with a clubhouse that had a small locker room, a small golf shop, a large ballroom, and a small apartment. The golf professional and his family lived in the small apartment. His name was C.W. "Shanty" Hogan and his wife and daughter were Lera and Lera Ann. They became a very important part of my life as I grew up.

While we were waiting for caddie jobs we would hit golf balls down the second fairway of the golf course. There was no practice range so this was the only place to practice. All we had in the way of equipment were old golf bags and clubs given to us by the members. The golf course was closed on Mondays, so "Shanty" would allow the caddies to play. Those of us who liked to play golf would get to the golf course early in the morning and play until dark.

Until we could accumulate enough clubs for our own set, we would share clubs. If some of the caddies had clubs and others did not, the caddie without clubs had the "privilege" of carrying the bag. Many of the members took an interest in the caddies and would loan us clubs to play with on Monday. Two of the members who took a particular interest in me were Buster Tuttle and Mr. Bill White.

Buster Tuttle was a long haul truck driver who owned three trucks and handled the business end of dispatching the trucks. He drove one of the trucks as well. Mr. Bill White was a former major league catcher with the New York

Giants baseball team. He owned 3,000 acres of cotton farm land as well as the local cotton gin. Everyone called him Mr. Bill or Preacher. Mr. Bill was very religious, which was not unusual in the Bible Belt of the South.

He was a big supporter of Baylor University and Hardin-Simmons University. His daughter, Billie White, attended Hardin-Simmons University and married Bill Scott who later became the basketball coach at Hardin-Simmons. She ultimately became a member of the Board of Trustees at Hardin-Simmons. Baylor and Hardin-Simmons were the two largest Baptist universities in Texas.

As I said, Buster Tuttle was a truck driver, but he was also the best player in Lamesa. When I caddied for Buster or one of the other players in Buster's group, I would observe Buster very closely. When I had the opportunity to hit golf balls, I would try to emulate his golf swing. Buster was tall and lanky so he seemed a good model for me. Buster was one of two people who truly influenced how I developed my golf swing in the formative years.

After I had been working as a caddie for three or four years, "Shanty" offered me a job as the water boy at the golf course. This job entailed watering the greens at night after play had been completed. The golf course did not have an automatic irrigation system so I had to walk the course four times each night. The first time I walked the course I would have to unwind the irrigation hoses and set the sprinkler on the corner of the green and turn it on. By the time I had walked all nine holes setting the sprinklers it was time to start over again. Each time I walked around the course setting the sprinklers took about an hour and a half.

After I had completely watered the greens I walked the course one final time and set the sprinklers on the tees. If I started watering greens at six o'clock I would usually finish about two thirty or three o'clock in the morning. Lamesa Country Club is located outside of town so I would have to walk three miles or so to get home.

One of the benefits of working for the club was that I could play golf during the day. I would sleep most of the morning, come to the golf course in the afternoon, and play golf until it was time to start my watering job. This gave me the opportunity to work on my game at an age in which it was easy to develop a good golf swing.

I think it is important to note that my job as a caddie and as water boy were summer jobs when school was out. During the school year I would work after school at the Piggly Wiggly grocery store, bagging groceries for the customers. After the store closed I would help restock the shelves and sweep the floor with a large push broom prior to going home. Again I had to walk home, a distance of a couple of miles.

As I got older and began high school, "Shanty" gave me a job working in the golf shop. During the summer I would work each day from eight in the morning until closing time. During the school year I would work on Saturday and Sunday in the golf shop. At all the small golf courses in West Texas, the golf professional was in charge of all phases of the course operation. This included maintenance of the course, running of the golf shop, and overseeing the locker room, as well as supervising any food and beverage operations. In the case of Lamesa Country Club, we had a small golf shop where we registered players, sold golf merchandise, primarily balls and gloves, as well as sandwiches and soft drinks.

We had a small locker room which was left unattended, but members could keep their shoes and clothing in their lockers. We also had a large ballroom where we held dances and other club functions. When we had the dances and other functions we would have the food and beverages catered. At this point in time in Texas, most of the state was dry, meaning there was no liquor or beer permitted to be sold on the premises. Anyone coming to the dances or other functions had to bring their own beverages. Being a professional at a small golf course in West Texas was a full time job at best, and sometimes would require the attention of the golf professional well into the night. It was essentially a twenty four hours a day, seven days a week job.

I want to explain a little about my family and our structure. I don't remember my mother or dad ever telling me or any of my brothers and sister that they loved us. From the way I talk about them, you may get the feeling that they did not love us. However, I am sure that they did. I think this is simply the reflection of the time and place where I grew up. I don't remember any of my brothers or my sister ever saying that we loved each other. To this day, I have not had any of them tell me they love me. I think it was something that was just not done. I think everyone just assumed that they were loved. The attitude was one for all and all for one. The focus of the family was for everyone to do their share to put a roof over our head, food on the table, and clothes on our back.

Before I was born, my family led a nomadic life. My dad and mom had a covered wagon that was home to them and my two older brothers. My dad had a fresno that was used to dig burn pits for oil wells as they were being drilled. This required them to move from drill site to drill site so mobility was necessary.

During World War II, our family moved around a lot. Since my dad had such a large family he was not drafted into the military. Because he had construction skills, we would move to different towns in the area where military facilities were being built. During the war we lived in Seagraves, Texas, Roswell, New Mexico, Big Springs and Seminole, Texas. Air Bases were being built in Roswell and Big Springs, and a carbon black plant in Seagraves.

Our first move was to Seminole and my mother would not move unless my dad agreed to move our house. She had bought the house when she inherited a small amount of money from her father when he died. His ranch was sold and the proceeds were split between her and her seven brothers and sisters. She was afraid that if we sold the house we would never own a home again.

Probably the most memorable thing that happened to our family during the war was the death of my Uncle Elmo. He was my mother's youngest brother. He joined the Army as soon as the war started. He was killed on Guadalcanal where his job was to locate land mines and defuse them. His truck, loaded with mines, was hit by lightning during a heavy rainstorm. Nothing was left of the truck or the passengers. The Army named a bridge on Guadalcanal in his honor. I often thought that I would like to visit that bridge, but during the years I was traveling in that part of the world, I never took the time to make the trip.

# *Decade of the 50's*

## A Close Call

After my sophomore year of College at Hardin-Simmons University in Abilene, Texas, I turned professional and became the Assistant golf professional at Abilene Country Club. I had been working in the golf shop at the club on weekends during the school year and full time during the summer. When Gervis McGraw, the assistant golf pro, left to take a position at Southern Hills Country Club in Tulsa, Oklahoma, Morgan Hampton, the golf professional at Abilene Country Club, offered me the position as his assistant. Even though I was on a full golf scholarship at Hardin-Simmons, it was not a difficult decision to take Morgan's offer. From the time I had been a junior golfer, my plan was to be a professional. When the opportunity presented itself, I felt it was too good to pass up.

A part of my compensation was the use of a small apartment which was located on the back of the driving range. The building had been built to serve as an operations center for the range but later it had been determined that it was not economically feasible to have a full time employee at the range. So, the building was converted to an apartment for me.

Jackie Clark, one of my teammates on the golf team at Hardin-Simmons, was hired to take my place as a shop assistant on weekends during the school year. Jackie's father was the golf professional at the Marlin Country Club in Marlin, Texas. Morgan felt that Jackie would be a great addition to our staff because of his experience working for his father for many years.

Because we had to open the golf shop at seven on Saturday and Sunday mornings, Jackie would spend Friday and Saturday nights with me so he would not have to travel all of the way across town early in the morning. Jackie did not have a car so I would usually pick him up on Friday evening. We would go to the movie and come out to my apartment to spend the night. I would take him back to the HSU campus after work on Sunday.

One Saturday night, Jackie and I went to a movie after having dinner and came back to my apartment to spend the night. The next morning we did not show up for work when we were due. This was highly unusual because we were always on time. However, the two other people that worked in the golf shop did not think too much of our absence. They just figured we had a hard night so they opened up and went ahead with business as usual.

When Morgan Hampton arrived about nine, he asked where we were and was told we had not arrived at work yet. Morgan sent one of the shop attendants to check on Jackie and me. Morgan usually went to the first tee on weekends and started the players. This gave him an opportunity to visit with the members.

The attendant found Jackie and me unconscious. I was on the floor and Jackie was in the bed. He ran to tell Morgan. As luck would have it one of the members on the first tee was Dr. Dub Sibley. Morgan told the attendant to call the police and he and Dr. Sibley ran to the apartment.

The pilot light on the water heater had blown out and gas had escaped into our bedroom. I was tall and skinny and Jackie was short and rotund. Dr. Sibley said it was a miracle we had survived. He said because I had fallen to the floor I did not get as much gas as Jackie. He also said that because Jackie was rotund his body could absorb more gas; otherwise both of us would have died.

Fortunately, Dr. Sibley was able to provide treatment until the paramedics arrived. We spent a couple of days in the hospital and were released in good shape. Dr. Sibley told me many times over the years how lucky we were to survive. He also said we were very fortunate there was not an explosion when they first entered the apartment with all of the gas accumulation in the bedroom. One spark was all it would have taken.

Just think, I was just minutes away from ruining a wonderful career.

## My College Buddy, Doyle Brunson

Doyle Brunson and I have been friends for a long time. We played basketball against each other in high school when he played for Sweetwater High School and I played for Lamesa. When I arrived at Hardin-Simmons University to play on the golf team, he was there to play basketball as well as to participate on the track team. Little did we know of the twist and turns our careers would take.

Doyle was one of the best athletes ever to attend Hardin-Simmons. By the time he had finished his junior year, he was being touted as a potential All-American in basketball. The Minneapolis Lakers professional basketball team had indicated an interest in drafting him in the NBA draft. Between his junior and senior years he secured a job at a sheetrock manufacturing plant in Sweetwater. While there, a stack of sheetrock fell on him, crushing his leg. He would spend his senior year on crutches in a cast.

The golf team had been assigned housing in an old army barracks located a couple of blocks off campus. These barracks were used to house several other university teams, including the basketball team. As happens on most college campuses, gin and poker games quickly started up in the barracks. A lot of the athletes participated in these games. Athletes are fiercely competitive and they find other games to play that challenge that competitive spirit. Many of these athletes took up golf to satisfy this need for competition.

25

Because we were on the golf team, we were asked to help them with their golf games. I was one who helped them improve their game and in return they would caddie for us in our matches. College is where Doyle developed his golf skills – as well as his poker skills.

Because his broken leg restricted his activity, poker became a great diversion for Doyle. Also, without his basketball scholarship, he needed to make some extra income to pay his way through school. This is when he really began his professional life as a poker player. After he got out of school, he tried to be a salesman for Burroughs Office Machines but found out very quickly that he was not happy with that career path. He discovered that he could make a living playing poker so that became his full time vocation. His autobiography, "The Godfather of Poker," is a great read about the incredible life he has lived. Doyle and I kept in touch with each other over the years because of our friendship in school as well as his love for golf.

In 2008, I had to go to Las Vegas for some PGA Meetings. When I found out I would be there for three days, I called Doyle Brunson to see if we could get together and talk about old times at Hardin-Simmons and what had happened in his world since we had last talked. He immediately agreed and told me to call him when I knew what night I was going to be free.

After two full days of meetings, I returned to my hotel and called Doyle. He told me he was at the Bellagio Hotel in the poker room and invited me to come over. He warned me not to be surprised when we walked through the casino because in Vegas he was like a "rock star." When I arrived, the gate keeper told me Doyle was in a meeting and asked if he was expecting me. I told him I had just talked to Doyle and he invited me to meet him here. He went and told Doyle I was there, who said to send me over to the meeting room. After we greeted each other and he introduced me to the other people in the room, he continued his meeting.

He would ask me a question and we would talk for a few minutes and then he would go back to his discussion.

As we made our way through the casino he was stopped constantly by people wanting his autograph and to talk to him. Brunson is a "rock star" in Vegas. He reminded me of Arnold Palmer in the way he interacted with the people. He would not only sign the autographs, he would stop and talk. He was very proud of the way he dealt with the people and said if they had that much interest in him he owed it to them to spend a little time with each one. He was just like the PGA tour players: he carried a Sharpie in his pocket for the autographs!

During dinner we had a wide-ranging conversation about our careers. I knew that he had played in a lot of big money golf games over the years. I was interested in knowing about some of them. I asked him what was the most money he played for in any match. He told me that his biggest match was a $250,000 Nassau bet with automatic two down presses and presses to get even at the end of each nine holes. I wanted to know the best score he had ever shot. He told me it was a 67 at Brackenridge Park Golf Course in San Antonio, Texas.

That idea started as he was playing in a poker game in Waco, Texas, when the conversation turned to golf. Two of the players in the game told him to get a partner and they would play a four ball match. Doyle told then he did not know anyone in the area to get as a partner. One of the other poker players said he was a pretty good player and would love to be Doyle's partner. He told Doyle he could shoot about 80. So the game was arranged to be played at Brackenridge Park in San Antonio. Doyle said when he saw his partner hit his first tee shot he knew he was in trouble. He said he had to shoot 67 to get out of the trap.

He asked me about the best score I ever had. I told him my best score was a 64, also shot at Brackenridge Park, to lead the first round of the 1957 Texas Open. It is strange that both of our best rounds were shot at the same course.

When I was President of the PGA, Doyle called me wanting the PGA to endorse a golf tournament he was trying to promote. His idea was that each player would put up their own money for the purse. The entry fee would be $100,000 per player of the player's own money. He thought it would be interesting to see how the players played when their own money was at risk. He had proposed the tournament to Deane Beman the PGA Tour Commissioner. Beman would not approve the tournament and said he would suspend any player who played in the event. I told him we could not approve the tournament but we would not disapprove it either. He did play the tournament for a few years but none of the tour players participated. He told me Lee Trevino and Orville Moody came out and watched them play. Dan Jenkins was there to write about the tournament.

We talked about some of his poker games and I asked him if he had played in any games where the game had been robbed. He confirmed that he had played in such games and that all of the players simply let the robbers take the money and leave. He said that they had been robbed on the golf course by robbers who pulled a gun and took their money. It was the cost of doing business.

One other thing about the money was the way the money was handled. If they were playing a golf match, each player would bring their money in a bag. A lot of matches were played by the hole, and the winner of each hole was paid at the end of that hole. If a match was played for 9 or 18 holes the money was put up in advance and the person holding the money would give it to the winner at the end of the match.

Doyle told me how disappointed he was that he had not been elected to the Hardin-Simmons University Sports Hall of Fame. There had been several efforts to get him selected by his former teammates and others who thought he should be in the Hall of Fame. We finally achieved this goal in 2009 when he was elected to the Hall of Fame and inducted at a dinner during homecoming. This was the largest attendance I have ever seen at the Hall of Fame dinner. It was a wonderful night.

I wish I had thought to tape our dinner conversation. It was so wide-ranging and interesting that I cannot remember everything we talked about. It was just two friends sitting and talking about each other's journey through life. Both of our paths have been pretty interesting. Before we ended the dinner, Doyle asked me a question that I had often wanted to ask him. He wanted to know if I had ever been told when we were in college that he and I looked alike. I told him that it happened to me several times and I had always wondered if he had been asked the same question.

## Ben Hogan at Junior Tournament in Abilene

In the mid 1950's there was a national junior tournament conducted by the insurance industry. In order to play in the national championship tournament you had to win your state tournament. The insurance industry conducted state tournaments which served as the qualifying tournaments.

While I was living in Abilene, and attending Hardin-Simmons University, I worked in the golf shop at the Abilene Municipal Golf Course to earn money to help pay my way through school. The summer I worked at the Abilene Municipal course, we hosted the state insurance tournament. The tournament usually had a field of one hundred and fifty juniors and was considered one of the premier junior tournaments of the year. Because it was sponsored by the insurance industry, a tremendous number of insurance agents supported the tournament.

I don't know the individual or insurance company that made the arrangements, but Ben Hogan was persuaded to come to Abilene to conduct a clinic for the participants. The arrangement made with Ben Hogan was that he would not charge an appearance fee to work the clinic as long as no entry fee was charged to attend. However, if an admission fee was charged then his fee would be five thousand dollars. Obviously, everyone was very excited to see Ben Hogan and have the opportunity to watch him hit balls and give some insight into his philosophy of the golf swing.

I can still see Hogan drive down the hill into the parking lot in a powder blue Cadillac. He and a good friend, Pollard Simon, a real estate developer from Dallas, drove out from Fort Worth. When Ben lifted his leather golf bag out of the trunk, it made a big impression with me and most of the others who were there to watch the clinic, especially the junior golfers. I am sure several junior golfers started dreaming of a career as a professional golfer after seeing Hogan get his clubs out of that large blue Cadillac. Because I was working in the golf shop, I was introduced to Ben. This was my first time to meet him. Little did I know that I would develop a good relationship with him over the next few years.

In order to control the size of the gallery for the clinic, the event was not publicized. Only a few city officials and leaders in the golf community were privately invited and surprisingly, the gallery was very manageable. The clinic was held on the first tee of the golf course. We did not have a practice range so the first tee area was the best place available for a golf clinic.

One of the people who had been invited was Sammy Baugh, the great quarterback and punter for the Washington Redskins and Texas Christian University in Fort Worth. Ben and Sammy had developed a friendship over the years. Sammy was the football coach at Hardin-Simmons University. Sammy had a real passion for golf after his football career ended. He played golf at the municipal course. As Ben got into his clinic, he saw Sammy in the gallery. Sammy had been late arriving. Ben then did something so out of character for him that he caused everyone in the gallery to gasp. He told us he had always admired Sammy Baugh's swing and wanted to show everyone how Sammy hit the ball. He then proceeded to turn his cap around backward, spread his feet very wide apart, and took a vicious swing, hitting behind the ball and bouncing the club over the ball. This was so out of character for Hogan that the gallery was dumb founded. I never saw Ben do anything like that again. Ironically, one of the local photographers who had been invited to the clinic took a picture of Hogan's depiction of Sammy Baugh's swing and sold it to Sports Illustrated.

## Playing the Tour

An Abilene Country Club member, Carl Miles, asked me in 1955 if I wanted to play the Winter Tour and that he would sponsor me. So, I went out and played a few tournaments that winter. I started in Los Angeles and played through the Texas Open. I qualified for some tournaments and made a few cuts. Later in the year he said, "Do you want to play full time?"

I started playing full time beginning in January of 1956. That was before you had to have an Approved Tournament Players Card to play the tour. You just showed up at the tournament, signed up, and played the Monday qualifying. If you qualified you got into the tournament and if you made the cut you got to play in the tournament the next week. If you didn't make the cut you went to Monday qualifying again. This process did not apply to the exempt players.

Then in 1956, in the middle of the year they come to me and said, "You can't play anymore."

They said this to Bobby Maxwell, Dave Ragan, me, and a few of the other players. We asked them why and they said we were not Approved Tournament Players. We asked how you got to be an approved tournament player and they said you had to apply and be approved. One the biggest tournaments of the year, the Tam O'Shanter, was coming up in Chicago in a couple of weeks.

You had to have two PGA members sign your application.

On the tour

Fred Hawkins and Billy Maxwell signed my application. Jack Smith, the golf professional at Amarillo Country Club, was the Secretary of the PGA Texas Section, and the PGA Section had to approve you. So I called Jack and he said to send the application to him. I sent him the application and he signed it. Bobby and I were approved in a week. We missed one tournament but we became approved tournament players and played the Tam O'Shanter the following week. That was exactly the time that the decision was made that a player had to be affiliated with the PGA in order to play the PGA tour. It was kind of interesting that the rule was implemented in the middle of the year.

In 1957, I shot a 64 in the first round of The Texas Open and led the tournament. This was great because it was in my home state. I had a number of rounds where I shot good scores. I was in second place after two rounds in Pensacola. I was a pretty good player, but by today's standards, we didn't have that much experience when we went on the tour. We played college golf but not nearly the amount they do today. We had no junior golf to speak of, so we had to come out on the tour to learn how to play. I might have been successful if I could have stayed on the tour and played longer. I was finished playing at twenty-two years of age. I started working on the tour when I was twenty-three.

At that young age, I was out there helping run the tour and I quit when I was thirty-one.

## Hardy Loudermilk

Hardy Loudermilk is a member of both the Texas Golf Hall of Fame as well as the PGA of America Hall of Fame. He was also selected as the Golf Professional of the Year in 1968. The interesting thing about Hardy is his journey to the top in his chosen profession.

In 1955 Hardy worked for Greyhound Bus Lines. He was living in Abilene, Texas. Because of his job, he had a lot of time off to play golf. He was a pretty good amateur player and competed in the amateur tournaments around West Texas when not working. He played at Abilene Country Club where I was the Assistant golf professional.

Hardy was in the process of getting a divorce and told me he was thinking about making a career change. He said he had always wanted to be a professional golfer and asked me to let him know if I heard of any job openings that might interest him.

Shortly after our conversation, I was approached by some members of Coleman Country Club about any interest I would have in becoming the Golf Professional at their club. I was getting ready to begin playing the PGA Tour so I told them I did not have any interest but I knew someone that I thought would do them a good job. I told them to get in touch with Hardy. After an interview, Hardy was selected as their professional. A couple of years later Hardy moved from Coleman to the position of Golf Professional at Jal Country Club in Jal, New Mexico.

In 1957, I was driving to my parents' home at Lamesa, from Tucson, Arizona, and had to pass through Jal. I called Hardy and told him I would stop by and have lunch with him. During lunch he told me he had a couple of junior golfers he would like me to see. He thought they had quite a bit of potential and would like my opinion. They were out on

33

the course playing so we drove out to watch them play a couple of holes. That is when I met Kathy Whitworth and Chris Blocker. Of course, Kathy became one of the greatest women professionals of all time and Chris played the men's tour, winning a couple of tournaments before quitting to purchase a golf course in Jacksonville, Florida, with Billy Maxwell.

Hardy moved from Jal to San Antonio, to become the Golf Professional at Oak Hill Country Club where he became one of the best in the country. Hardy developed a reputation for training young golf professionals. Several of the finest professionals in the country today got their start as an assistant to Hardy Loudermilk. Not bad for a fellow who started out as a Greyhound Bus Lines employee.

## Hogan and Crosby at Pebble Beach

Ben Hogan last played the Bing Crosby Clam Bake in 1956. This was also the last and only time I played in the Crosby. Ben was paired with Bing Crosby, and I was paired with Peanuts Lowery, the major league baseball player who later coached on Alvin Dark's coaching staff. At that time, the tournament was played on three courses, Cypress Point, Monterey Country Club Dunes Course, and Pebble Beach. All of the teams played 18 holes on each of the three courses and then a cut was made. The low fifteen teams and the low sixty professionals played the final round at Pebble Beach. Ben made the cut on his own ball and he and Bing made the cut as a team. The same was true with Peanuts and me.

The weather had been pretty good the first two days, but Sunday morning brought a huge Pacific front with strong winds and a driving rainstorm. Because I had played pretty well the first two days, and Peanuts and I had also played well as a team, we were paired in one of the last few groups. Ben and Bing were paired just ahead of Peanuts and me.

At that time, the Pebble Beach golf shop was a small building directly across from the first tee. There was a small changing room in the back of the golf shop where the players could change their shoes. Peanuts and I happened to be in the changing room at the same time that Ben Hogan and Bing Crosby were changing their shoes. Ben was quite upset that we were being required to play in this kind of weather. At that time on the tour, the Bing Crosby Clam Bake was not an official event, so the tour staff did not control the administration of the play of the event. The final decision about whether or not to play was in Bing Crosby's hands. Bing was delighted that the weather was so bad. He called it "Crosby Weather." He was laughing at Ben's protest about playing.

When we got to the first tee, we were told that the rules for the day were that we could improve our lie anywhere on the course, even in the bunkers. We were told there would be someone on each green to clean the water off of our line just prior to putting. Without a doubt that was the most miserable day I ever spent on a golf course. We were all wearing our rain suits but before we had played two holes we were totally soaked. The rain suits were worthless.

Because we were improving our lie on the course and had to wait while each player had their line cleared of water before putting, the round took six hours to play. Because we were playing so slow the tournament committee had people out on the course rushing us to play faster so we could finish before dark. I shot 83 on the last round and finished out of the money. Ben shot 81 and said he would never play at the Crosby tournament again. It was situations like this that motivated the PGA to take more control of the administration of the tour.

Was the course unplayable? Absolutely! It was unplayable before we began play. In one way, I was the benefactor of decisions like this. By the time I joined the PGA field staff we were pretty much in charge of all decisions pertaining to the golf course.

## A Life Changing Opportunity

I quit playing the tour in the spring of 1957 and took a job as the assistant golf professional to Vern Farquhar at Ross Rogers Golf Course in Amarillo, Texas. Ross Rogers is a 36 hole municipal course that sees lots of rounds of golf. It is open seven days a week from dawn to dark. Because I quit the tour in late spring, it was too late to find a seasonal job in the east, where I would be able to play the following winter tour. I was happy to find the job, because I was short of cash and needed to start generating some income as quickly as possible.

It was a great experience working for Vern and Grace Farquhar. Vern loved to sit on the couch in the clubhouse and tell stories and joke with the players as they arrived at the golf course. Grace was the one who really ran the golf course. Vern, Grace, and I got along very well from the beginning and developed a lifelong friendship.

As the fall season began, I started thinking about what direction I wanted my career path to take. I knew Vern and Grace would love for me to stay for another year or two before moving to a new position. However, I felt like Amarillo was pretty much a dead end if I did not pursue a new opportunity.

One day I received a call from a good friend of mine, Joe Zakarian. We had played together on the tour. He had recently left the tour to take a position in Detroit as a representative for a golf manufacturer. The season was over and he was on his way back home to Modesto, California. He was passing through Amarillo and wanted to know if I would like to get together for lunch and catch up on what was going on in our careers. At lunch, I told Joe of my concern about being stuck in Amarillo for another year. I told him to give me a call if he heard of any jobs in Detroit he thought I would be interested in.

A couple of weeks later I got a call from Harvey Raynor who was the Tournament Director for the PGA Tour. I knew Harvey from when I played the tour. At that time, he was Assistant Tournament Director, but he later replaced Ray O'Brien as Director. Harvey lived in Modesto and had seen Joe Zakarian when he arrived home from Detroit. He told Joe he was looking for an Assistant, thinking Joe might be interested in the position, but Joe declined.

He told Harvey that he had seen me in Amarillo and that I might be interested. Harvey offered me the job on the phone. I told him I would think about it and call him back in a couple of days. After telling Vern and Grace of the call, I decided to take the position. When I called Harvey back, he told me to pick up a new Pontiac station wagon in Tulsa after Christmas and be in Los Angeles the week before the New Year. Little did I know this would change my life forever. My plans were to work a couple of years on the tour and then hopefully secure a position in New York. I thought the Tour position would look good on my resume. Life takes some strange twists and turns.

## Bob Goalby at Greensboro

I arrived in Los Angeles about nine one evening and had a reservation at The Back Motel. When I went to check in, the clerk said, "Oh, your buddy has already checked in."

I said "What do you mean my buddy has already checked in?"

He said, "Your buddy came in and wanted a room and I said we didn't have one for him. When I told him you had a room reservation, he said, 'Oh I will just stay with him.'"

It turned out to be Bob Goalby. It was his second tournament on the tour. He had played at Sanford, Florida, the last tournament on the fall tour, made the cut, and was exempt at Los Angeles. That was the first time I met Goalby. We roomed together a lot that first year. He played really well all winter.

When I would get to a tournament and do an interview the media would ask, "Who are the best young players?"

I would invariably say, "Well I've got to go with Goalby".

We got to Wilmington a week before the Masters and he was supposed to go back to Connecticut where he was an Assistant Pro at Darien Country Club. He had just come out to play the Winter Tour. He got to Wilmington and played really well, made some money, and signed a contract with Spalding. They paid him a little money to use their equipment.

Then he had a big decision to make – should he keep playing the tour or go back to his job? So, I asked him if he wanted to commit to the Greensboro tournament the week after the Masters. He said he was going on to Darien and if he called me to enter the Greensboro Tournament he would be playing the tour full time.

He called me and entered Greensboro, won the tournament and the rest is history.

## Havana Country Club

The last tournament of the year in 1958 was the Havana Invitational at Havana Country Club in Havana, Cuba. This was an invitation-only event with the top forty players from the 1958 money list invited. There was a purse of $50,000.00 for the tournament, with all of the players guaranteed a minimum payoff. The players' expenses were also paid. All of the players were permitted to bring their wives if they desired.

The Havana Country Club was a very exclusive club located a short distance outside the city of Havana. The Club had twenty sleeping rooms. This was not unusual with clubs built in the 1930's and 1940's. All of the players and officials who brought their wives were put up at the Club. The single players were housed at the Havana Hilton, which was a resort and casino on the water in downtown Havana.

1958 was a very volatile year in Havana. Fidel Castro was trying to overthrow the Batista Government and was advancing on Havana. The tournament was being played the week before Christmas, and Castro was expected to arrive on the outskirts of Havana just after the first of the year. We had a lot of concern about playing in Havana with the political situation. However, Jack Sendoya, the Tournament Chairman, assured us it would not be dangerous. Because

1958 Havana Invitational

of the situation, we decided we would require the purse money to be placed in escrow in our bank in Florida before we would agree to play the tournament. I have thought many times over the years about how stupid we were to require the money be deposited in Florida and then get on an airplane and go to Cuba.

We flew from West Palm Beach to Havana on a charter flight. When we arrived, Jack Sendoya boarded the plane prior to our deplaning and told me he wanted to talk to our group about the political situation in Cuba. He told us that we were not to discuss the Cuban situation with any of the members. The members had agreed to not discuss the situation while at the club. He said most of the members do not know which side the other members may be supporting. He said if a member had a few drinks and began expressing their support for one side or the other, he may not show up to play the next day.

The week was uneventful except for one incident involving Julius Boros, Bill Collins, and George Bayer. The three were very good friends and had a habit of having dinner and hanging out together most of the time. One night during the tournament, the three, who were staying at the Havana Hilton, decided to remain at the club and have dinner with their amateur partners. After dinner they took a cab back into the hotel. On route to the hotel, their cab was stopped by the military. A machine gun was poked into the window of the cab and they were told to get out of the car. The cab was searched by the military officers looking for weapons they thought the guys might be smuggling into the city. These three men were three of the biggest guys on the tour but they said they were as meek as lambs during this incident.

History shows that Castro took over Cuba the first of January, 1959 – two weeks after we returned to the United States.

## Fish Story

The PGA Tour played a tournament in Vancouver British Columbia, Canada, in 1958. The tournament was to celebrate the 100th anniversary of the city. It was appropriately called the Vancouver B.C. Centennial Open, and was played at Point Grey Country Club. Jim Ferree captured his only win on the PGA Tour at the tournament. He opened with an 11 under par 61, and held a six stroke lead after the first round. He was never really challenged. The point of the story is not Jim's win, which was a great accomplishment with one of the lowest scores in tour history at that time. Nor is it to document Jim winning his first and only tour victory. This story is about the unusual circumstances surrounding the playing of the event.

At that time, Canada had a law which was referred to as the Blue Law. The law provided that a sporting event could not begin before 1:00 p.m. on Sunday. It was decided that we would play the tournament on Thursday, Friday and Saturday, skip Sunday, and complete the event on Monday. In order to be good hosts, the local tournament committee decided to invite all of the players who made the cut to go on a yacht cruise with fishing provided for those who wanted to try their hand at trying to catch a salmon.

We were playing the tournament in September so the weather was cool. When we boarded the yacht, it was rather blustery so most of the players decided to skip the fishing. Billy Casper and I decided to try to catch a salmon. Billy was a very experienced fisherman who carried fishing gear with him when he traveled on the tour. Being from San Diego, Billy had fished in the ocean many times. I had been fishing only a couple of times, and never in the ocean. After we got out of the harbor and the crew rigged up the fishing gear, we got busy trying to catch a salmon. As the day wore on, the weather began to deteriorate and the fishing became less and less fun. However, just before we were about to call it quits I caught a 65 pound salmon. It was a great thrill for me and gave me some bragging rights on Billy and the rest of the guys.

When the crew came to me and asked what I wanted to do with the fish, I did not know what to say. I had not thought that far ahead. I asked the crew if they would like to have the fish and they were delighted. They said they would make a great meal out of it.

## Placing the Rake in the Bunker

At first look, you would not think the USGA Rules of Golf Committee would care where the bunker rake would be placed on the course. However, it became a hotly debated subject at few committee meetings while I was serving on the committee representing the PGA of America as a consulting member. The PGA Tour representative was Clyde Mangum, who was the Director of Rules and Competition for the tour. At that time I was the Chairman of the PGA Rules Committee.

At one of the meetings of the Rules of Golf Committee, I raised the question of where the bunker rake should be left on the course. An immediate response came from several members of the committee with several different points of view offered. Most of the committee members felt that the rake should be placed outside the bunker in an area that would not interfere with play. My argument to this opinion was that it would slow down play. The player would have to walk to the out of play area to retrieve the rake, walk to the area in the bunker that needed repair, and then return the rake to the out of play area. If this were the procedure it would slow down play substantially.

There was even a suggestion that rakes be carried by the player on his golf cart or on his pull cart if the player did not ride a golf cart. This suggestion received no support because it had not been thought through very well. First, many players would not be using a riding cart or using a pull cart, and it would be very inconvenient for the player walking and carrying his bag. Even though the idea of carrying a rake on the golf cart was rejected, some of the golf cart manufacturers produced carts with a rake holder.

It was suggested that players would forget the rake and leave it on the cart, or not realize when they were in a bunker that they did not bring the rake with them. They would then have to go back to their cart for the rake or simply not rake the bunker.

My suggestion was that the rake be placed in the bunker in proximity to the area where most of the balls would be found in the bunker. My thinking was that the rake was going to be used in the bunker, so place it where it was to be used. If the rake were in the bunker and the ball hit the rake it would probably stay in the bunker so the player would not gain any advantage. If the ball hit the rake outside the bunker, the ball may stay outside the bunker, which would give the player an advantage by keeping the ball outside of the bunker. It also would not be fair to the other players in the competition for the player to gain an advantage that could adversely affect the other players.

Clyde Mangum argued that the rake should be placed outside of the bunker and I argued for the rake being placed in the bunker. After a lot of discussion, a vote of the committee was called and the committee voted to recommend the rake be placed in the bunker at the area where the rake would most likely be used. This recommendation was put in the Rules of Golf Book and followed for several years. However, when I finished my term on the committee, Clyde Mangum raised the issue again and got the committee to change the recommendation to place the rake outside the bunker. Several years after Clyde went off of the committee, they again voted to return the rake to the bunker.

## Driving a New Pontiac

Walter Burkemo, the 1953 PGA Champion, was also the golf professional at Franklin Hills Country Club in Birmingham, Michigan. Several of the members at Franklin Hills were top executives at Pontiac Motor Division of General Motors. Walter convinced some of the Pontiac Executives that it would be a great promotion to have the top 40 money winners on the tour and me and my staff drive the Pontiac Grand Prix on the tour.

At each tournament there is special parking lot at the Clubhouse for the players and officials. They thought it would look great to have all of the top players and my staff drive into the parking lot in the Grand Prix each day. All of the cars were to be white, which would really stand out, and they would be on display all day. As with all good plans, the actions of a few can ruin a good arrangement for the participants.

There were a few incidents that caused Pontiac to finally cancel the deal. Some of the players would not drive their cars, but would have their caddie drive for them while they flew between tournaments. Obviously, the Pontiac folks were not too happy seeing caddies drive up to the club in the players' car. This was not a deal breaker but it certainly did not help.

One of the worst incidents was caused by a player who was taking a couple of weeks off and let his caddie drive the car while he was off the tour. The caddie drove the car to Jackson, Mississippi, and parked it in the parking lot at the airport, and left it there. When the player came back on tour in a couple of weeks, he had no caddie and no car. The player did not have any way of contacting the caddie so we had to report the car stolen. Several weeks later the car was located by the authorities when they were doing a parking lot check. The caddie never showed back up on the tour.

The arrangement with Pontiac provided that we would drive the car about 6,000 miles and trade it in for a new car. The Pontiac people thought that the swap of cars would take place at one place with all of the players. Unfortunately, all of the players do not play all of the tournaments, so the swap usually had to take place over two or three weeks, which caused a logistical nightmare for Pontiac. To compound the problem, some of the players would commit to trade out their car at a specific tournament then withdraw at the last minute and leave Pontiac high and dry.

However the incident that broke the camel's back involved a couple of players who came up with the bright idea of going home the week before they were supposed to trade cars and change the tires from their personal car with the tires from the Pontiac. When confronted with this they said they did not think that it would be noticed. Unbelievable!!

At that time, almost everyone on the tour drove all of the time, so it was a huge financial loss to most of those who were fortunate enough to participate in the program. I personally drove about 50,000 miles a year, so I had to buy a new car each year. I saved the cost of a new car each year and had no insurance costs, as those were paid by Pontiac. It was also really nice to be able to drive five or six new cars a year.

## Tommy Bolt at Southern Hills

The 1958 U.S. Open at Southern Hills Country Club in Tulsa, Oklahoma, was the first Open Championship I ever attended. I was not there in any official capacity as far as conducting the play of the Championship was concerned. I was there representing the PGA and the players and to help the players if they had any need for assistance. I was also there in case any of the players wanted to commit to play in any of the future events on the tour.

Even though the Open is played in June, the weather was very hot, as it can be at any time during the spring and summer in Oklahoma. Hot weather seems to wear on the players. As a result, some of the players are on edge and tempers can become a little short.

Tommy Bolt was the first round leader, and the headlines in the paper Friday morning read, "49 YEAR OLD TOMMY BOLT LEADS OPEN."

Tommy was livid when he saw that headline. As soon as he arrived at the golf course on Friday, he went to the Press Room to confront the writer who had written the story. When Tommy told the writer of his displeasure and that he was 39 instead of 49, the writer said, "but Tommy, that was a typographical error."

Tommy replied, "Typographical error hell! That was a perfect 4 and a perfect 9!"

For the balance of the tournament, Tommy would not go to the Press Room after his round. There was a golf Writer from Rochester, New York, named Bruce Koch, who was a friend of Tommy. Bruce would sit in the locker room with Tommy and do an interview and then go to the Press Room and conduct the interview with the media. Tommy won the 1958 U.S. Open.

## Significant Events in Golf – 1950-59

**Arnold Palmer** -- Without a doubt, the most important event in golf in the 50's was when Arnold Palmer joined the PGA Tour. With Arnold's infectious personality and swash buckling style of play, he became an American hero almost instantly. With the advent of golf on television and the incredible things he did as soon as the camera came on, he became a man of the people. He had the innate ability to connect in a special way with the gallery as well as the television audience. He attracted the common man to the game. He drew huge galleries and television ratings to tournament golf. That's why he is called the "King."

**Mark McCormack and IMG** -- Mark McCormack was a young attorney from Cleveland, Ohio. Mark was convinced that with the emergence of television in sports there was an opportunity to form a company to represent professional athletes in pursuing business opportunities outside of the game. Mark approached Arnold Palmer with his idea and Palmer agreed to let McCormack represent him in negotiating business opportunities, including endorsement agreements, exhibitions, books, television appearances, and any other opportunities that Mark could find, as long as Arnold felt comfortable with the relationship. Thus International Management Group was formed. The deal was signed with a hand shake and a formal contract was never prepared. Soon, McCormack signed Gary Player and Jack Nicklaus and started marketing them as golf's big three.

IMG became a worldwide organization with offices around the globe, attracting clients in other sports, especially tennis. They also manage sports events, negotiate television contracts for various sports organizations, and represent such diverse entities as Wimbledon and the Pope. Mark McCormack dramatically changed the economic opportunities of the professional golfer as well as other sports.

**Real Estate Golf Development** -- There had always been a certain number of real estate golf developments, but they were primarily driven by individuals or groups who were trying to develop a country club. They also provided property around the club for the members to build homes. As the game of golf began to grow, real estate developers and home builders changed that model. They created huge developments with a country club as one of the amenities that buyers of homes in the development could join. The idea was to sell the development as a life style, providing family entertainment where they lived. These clubs usually had a golf course, swimming pool, and tennis facility, as well as food and beverage service. Later athletic facilities were added as the health craze became more prominent. The club would develop programs that were attractive for the members, such as golf and tennis tournaments, swim teams for the kids, parties at the club for the members, and professional staffs to teach the members who were not engaged in these activities.

**Bob Dedman and CCI** -- Bob Dedman was a young attorney in Dallas who had H.L. Hunt and the American Football League as clients. He was aware of the new method of selling real estate by using golf as an amenity. He knew that most of the developers were not interested in retaining ownership of the golf facilities after they had sold the real estate. Bob had two ideas that he wanted to pursue as it related to the country club developments. One concept was to build multiple golf courses as a part of the development. The idea being that two or three courses, operated out of one clubhouse facility with one professional staff, would provide the opportunity to sell memberships for a lesser fee and lower monthly dues.

Because there were more facilities, there would also be the opportunity to sell more memberships to the club. "A Cadillac facility at Chevrolet prices," became the marketing theme. Bob felt that this concept would provide middle class Americans the opportunity to enjoy the country club life style because the lower fees would fit into their budget.

The other part of Bob's concept was that Country Clubs should be run by professional management, not by a Board of Directors. He wanted to develop a management and marketing model that could be duplicated at facilities around the country. He believed that management training programs could be implemented at the clubs so that when a new club was developed or acquired, he would have people trained in his management and marketing concepts to install into the new facility.

Bob had no interest in participating in the real estate part of the development, only in the ownership and management of Country Clubs. He was filling a void for the real estate developer. CCI later changed its name to Club Corporation of America and then shortened it to CCA. CCA became the largest owner and manager of Country Clubs in the world and the model for the development of several golf management companies.


**Golf Cars** -- The development of the golf car was one of the most profound advances for golf in the 1950's. The golf car was created to satisfy a need for players who could not play golf for physical reasons, and people who did not want to carry their own clubs. Some thought it would speed up the game. The first golf cars were small automobiles with

48

their tops cut off and a rack built on the back for the clubs. The most popular small car used initially was the Crosby automobile. It was small and easy to convert.

It did not take long for the profit motive to come into play with the advent of the golf car. Several golf car manufacturing companies came into being to satisfy this new phenomenon. EZ-GO, based in Augusta, Georgia, soon became the leading golf car manufacturer. At first, the local golf professional was given the concession to provide golf cars at the golf facilities. He either bought or leased the cars to rent to his golfers. Some clubs allowed members to own their own cars. Developers even used car ownership as a perk for those buying homes in their developments. Finally the clubs themselves saw the golf car revenue as a way to help defray the operating cost of the club. Now, most retain the car operation as a responsibility of the club and retain the income for club use.

When I first started working on the tour in 1958, there were some golf courses that did not have golf cars so we had to get the tournament sponsor to lease some cars or borrow them from a nearby club for the week to be brought in for our use during the tournament. At the 1958 Los Angeles Open, they did not have golf cars and could not borrow or lease any for the week, so we had to drive our automobiles around the maintenance roads through the course and then walk or run across the course to answer a call for a ruling.

**Pairing System** -- As the PGA Tour became more prominent in the 1950's, there were several things done to create a more equitable system for conducting the play of the tournaments. One of the biggest improvements was in the way the pairings were made. In the early day of the tour, the sponsor would have a lot of input into the pairings. They would want to pair certain prominent players together and tee them off at the time they felt would attract the most spectators. There was not a lot of thought given to the equity of the system for all of the players in the tournament.

Several of the players started complaining about the arbitrary system being used. Howard Capps, who was the Tournament Director at the time, developed a system that was far more equitable and was adopted for all future tour tournaments. The system worked as follows and is essentially still used today.

The players are divided into various categories depending on their playing records. The different categories are Current Tournament Winners, Former Tournament Winners, Major Money Winners who have not won a tournament, Lesser Money Winners, and the balance of the field. Each player's name is written on a 3 x 5 index card and divided into various piles depending on their category. The cards are shuffled like a deck of cards and dealt out in groups of threes.

The groups in each category are divided into two halves. For the first two days, the three players in each group will play together, with one assigned tee time in the morning and one tee time in the afternoon. The tee times determined for the first two days are divided in half and the times to be assigned to the various categories are determined. Half of the groups are assigned to the morning times and half to the afternoon times.

After the first round the groups that played in the morning will play in the afternoon and vice versa for the second round. All of this is done with the cards placed face down so that no one knows where players are drawn until their times have been assigned.

This system assures that the players in each category have one early and one late time, and that the players in each category play at the corresponding time to their counterpart. After the second round as the players finish their round, their scores are recorded on their 3 x 5 card and placed in order of their score in the deck. If two players playing together shoot the same score, the player that teed off first on the first hole is posted first and placed in the deck first. Once the cut score has been determined, the players who have made the cut are separated out and their card is dealt out face down, with players one and two paired together, and three and four together, and this procedure is followed through the deck until all cards are laid out. The pair with the two lowest scores will tee off last and the players with the highest scores will tee off first. This same procedure is followed for the final round.

# Decade of the 60's

## E.J. "Dutch" Harrison

Dutch Harrison was not only a very fine player on the PGA Tour in the 1950's and 1960's, but also one of the more colorful characters in golf. Prior to playing the tour, Dutch had done a little hustling with his golf game. He also loved horse racing. Any time the tour was near a racetrack, you could always depend on Dutch and Porky Oliver being in attendance every spare moment. Dutch was a great storyteller and at different times told me many of his stories. I always thought the following one was funny.

When Dutch was young, he and some of his buddies would go to the racetrack in Hot Springs, Arkansas, at every opportunity. They would sit in the grandstands and try to find a group of "little old ladies" to sit behind. They knew that these ladies would always bet the long shots hoping to get a big payoff. If one of the ladies would hit a winner, they would usually stand up and wave their winning ticket in the air and yell "I've got it! I've got it! I've got it!"

Dutch said they would stand up behind the lady, grab the winning ticket out of her hand, and run off yelling, "You had it! You had it! You had it!"

Another trick that Dutch used quite often was one that I observed many times. Dutch was tall and had a very unique swing.  He took the club to the outside of his line and rerouted it to the inside. The swing was very smooth and he could hit a shot with a 2 iron, 210 yards or 190 yards with the same swing. His swing was so smooth that most people could not tell the difference in the speed of the swing. If he was paired with one of the new young players on the tour and he had the honors on a long par 3, he would make a big production of selecting the club for the shot. There would be a lot of communication with his caddie before deciding which club to use. He would take that big smooth swing of his and put the ball right on the green. The young player would take a similar club and hit his shot toward the hole and I would try to be sitting behind the green in my cart to watch the ball sail over my head.

## Jack Nicklaus at the Cape Fear Open

Jack Nicklaus won the 1959 U.S. Amateur Championship and as a result was invited to play in the 1960 Masters Tournament. Jack was a student at Ohio State University and did not have many opportunities to play or practice because of the winter weather. Jack wanted to get in some competitive golf prior to the Masters Tournament, so he called to see if I would help him get an invitation to the 1960 Cape Fear Open, played at Cape Fear Country Club in Wilmington, North Carolina.

The sponsor of a tour tournament at that time could invite four players as sponsor's exemptions under their contract with the PGA. These players could be either amateurs or professionals. If professionals, they did not have to be members or approved tournament players of the PGA. I called "Bunny" Heins who was the Tournament Chairman for the Cape Fear Open and asked him if he wanted to invite Jack to the tournament.

Being the week before The Masters Tournament made it difficult to attract a lot of the top players who opted to go to Augusta early and practice for the Masters Tournament. "Bunny" and I both thought Jack would be a great addition because it would attract additional media attention with the U.S. Amateur Champion in the field. So the invitation was extended.

One other top amateur in the country had been invited to play at The Masters and had also been invited to play at

Wilmington. At that time there were 144 players starting the tournament with the field cut to the top 60 players and ties after the first two rounds of the tournament. It was not too common for the cut to be an even 60 players, but that is what happened at Wilmington.

Jack Nicklaus played well enough to make the cut but not well enough to be considered a serious contender to win the tournament. After the second round was completed and the cut of the low 60 players announced, I made the pairings for the third round of play. Our rules were that if a player made the cut but withdrew before the pairings were made, he would not count in determining the cut. If a player withdrew after the pairings were made, the cut would stand.

After the pairings were made, Jack called and told me he was withdrawing from the tournament. He said he and the other amateur were traveling together and since he did not want to stay around until Sunday when the tournament was over, they decided to go to Augusta and practice for the Masters Tournament.

This really upset me because I had asked "Bunny" Heins to give Jack an exemption into the tournament which took away a spot from a professional who was playing the tour for a living. Also, by not withdrawing before the cut, he had eliminated all of the players who would have made the cut and had a chance to make some money that week.

When I saw Jack at Augusta the next week, he and I had a little chat about the consequences of his withdrawal. I told him he put me in a very embarrassing position with "Bunny" Heins and I felt he owed all of the players who missed the cut an apology.

## Bob Goalby at The Masters

One year at The Masters Tournament, the weather was hot and dry and the greens were crusty from the dry wind.

There had been a couple of incidents where a player had putted his ball off of the ninth green because the conditions made the greens extremely fast. Needless to say, there was a lot of complaining about the conditions from the players who were having difficulty making putts. As a matter of fact, three putting was a pretty common occurrence. I was the rules official at the 18th hole as well as the one handling the scoring when the players finished their round.

Bob Goalby was a former winner of The Masters Tournament. On this particular day, the hole on the 18th green was on the left front of the green just over the bunker. The green was two tiered with a severe slope from the back to the front. Because of the dry conditions there were a lot of players who were finding their ball on the upper tier. This meant they had to putt back down the severe slope to the front hole position. This is the situation Bob Goalby found himself in after he played his second shot to the green.

After Bob marked his position and his caddy cleaned the ball, he replaced it where he had marked its position. He then began walking down the green toward the hole to try to judge the speed of the green and to also determine the break of the putt. As he walked away from the ball, it began to roll. It rolled right past Bob and came to rest a few inches from the hole. He was horrified. He did not know what to do so he called for an official to give him a ruling.

When he explained what had happened I told him there was no penalty and he would have to play the ball from where it came to rest a few inches from the hole. First he could not believe there was not a penalty and second could not believe he did not have to replace the ball back where it had come to rest up on the second tier of the green.

The rules provide that after a player has marked his ball and replaced it, the ball is in play. If the ball moves after it has been replaced, and the player has done nothing to cause the ball to move, the player will play the ball from where it comes to rest. In Bob's case this was a few inches from the hole. Bob tapped the ball in the hole for an easy birdie. Of course, if the ball had rolled off of the green or in the bunker he would have had to play the ball from there.

## Tommy Bolt and Jackie Burke in Tijuana

For a couple of years in the early 1960's, the PGA Tour played a tournament in Tijuana, Mexico, just across the border from San Diego. The tournament was sponsored by the Aqua Caliente beer company and was played at the course at the horse racing track. The tournament was named the Aqua Caliente Open after the beer company sponsor.

We had been having a problem with some of the players displaying an excessive amount of temper on the golf course. Consequently, we decided to impose a $100 fine for any outbreak of temper such as profanity or throwing clubs. It is well documented that Tommy Bolt was one of the biggest offenders when it came to throwing clubs.

For the first two rounds of the tournament, Tommy Bolt and Jackie Burke were paired together. Both players were from the Houston area and were quite familiar with each other. I think it would be fair to say that there was not a lot of love lost between the two players.

There was a long par four on the front nine that was probably one of the best holes on the course. Tommy hit a great second shot on this hole and had a very short putt for a birdie. This was before we started roping each hole individually. We only roped around the tees and greens. Tommy missed the short putt and in a fit of anger threw his putter over the heads of the gallery that had surrounded the green. He then turned to Jackie Burke and said, "I guess you are going to tell Joe Black on me for throwing that club."

Jackie said, "Just as soon as I see him."

A few holes later, Jackie saw me riding around the course in my golf cart and called for me to come over to where he and Bolt were playing. When I drove up to Jackie, he called Tommy over and said, "Joe, Tommy has a confession to make."

Jackie wasn't going to report Tommy for throwing the club but he was going to make Tommy report himself. Needless to say this did not endear Jackie to Tommy.

## President Eisenhower Money Clip

Prior to the Palm Springs Tournament being named the Bob Hope Classic it was called the Palm Springs Golf Classic. Over the years the tournament has been played on many different courses. At first, it was only 54 holes with a field of forty professionals. It was expanded to a full field tournament with 120 players in the mid 1950's. The courses being used at that time were Indian Wells Country Club, Bermuda Dunes Country Club, La Quinta Country Club, and Eldorado Country Club. The host course would rotate between the four clubs, which meant that the final round of the tournament would be played at the host club. The first four rounds were played as a pro-amateur with the final round played only by the professionals.

Former President Dwight Eisenhower had a condominium at Eldorado Country Club where he would spend time in the winter. Because of his great passion for golf, and the fact that he was usually in Palm Springs during the tournament, he was asked to donate his putter to become the trophy for the event. The putter was placed inside a shadow box and enclosed with a glass top. The five stars used to designate his rank in the army were placed on top of the shadow box to complete the trophy. General Eisenhower had sterling silver replica money clips of the trophy made, which he gave out as gifts. I was told there were twenty of the money clips produced. He gave me one as a memento of the tournament. The tournament was played at Eldorado Country Club that year.

We gave General Eisenhower a golf cart to use when he wanted to go out on the course to watch the play. He had a friend, Pollard Simon from Dallas, who was also a member at Eldorado who would drive him around the course. The final round of the tournament was played at Eldorado Country Club in 1964. Jimmy Demaret and Tommy Jacobs tied for the tournament which meant that we would have a sudden victory playoff.

As we were preparing for the playoff, General Eisenhower asked me if it would be alright if he followed the playoff in his cart. At that time we were not roping the fairways so it would have been very disruptive to have the former President out on the course in a golf cart among the gallery. I told him I would prefer that he not. He simply said, "Okay Joe, I will watch it on the TV in the clubhouse."

We had the playoff which was won by Tommy Jacobs.

It is not very often you get to tell the former President of the United States what he can or cannot do, and for him to be so gracious about it. However, it did not set too well with Pollard Simon. I knew Pollard because I also lived in Dallas. He came to me later and told me he thought it was terrible that I would not let General Eisenhower follow the playoff. I think Pollard was unhappy because he wanted to watch it himself.

## Tommy Bolt at Olympia Fields

We were playing the PGA Championship at Olympia Fields in 1961. That's when Don January and Jerry Barber had a playoff. Tommy Bolt was playing and I got a call on my radio that Bolt had walked off the golf course at the Par 3, 15th hole, so I went into the locker room looking for him. He did this all the time and it I was tired of him abusing the rules. I went in and found him, and he said, "Oh, Joe, I went as far as I could. My back's killing me. I tried and I just couldn't play anymore."

This was his excuse and he had a medical reason for not finishing, which was permitted. Well, we got rained out, and at that time when it was rained out, that round was cancelled and started over the next day. Therefore, anyone who withdrew or was cancelled had the right to play the next day. Tommy called me at the hotel that night and said "Hey, Joe, old buddy, I heard it was rained out today."

I said, "That's right, T."

"That means I can play tomorrow," he said.

And I replied, "That's right, T."

Then he said, "Okay!"

Then I felt it was necessary to say, "Let me tell you this. Don't you walk off that golf course tomorrow."

The next day, the same hole, I got a call, "Joe, Tommy just walked off the course."

So, I went into the locker room and I was really mad. When I found Tommy, a priest had just walked up to him and said something. Right there in the locker room, Tommy just cussed him out. That really got to me and I said, "T, you are out of the game. I am suspending you for life!"

At that time the tournament director handled everything; fines, suspensions, etc., that was part of our deal. We had guidelines, but ultimately it was our decision.

Of course he appealed my decision, but the Tournament Committee wasn't having another meeting for about six weeks at the World Series of Golf. That was when we were doing the television series called All Star Golf. Jack Tuthill or I would run the matches for Peter DeMet Productions. We would set up the golf course, handle the rulings, and conduct the play.

It happened that Tommy was playing in an All Star Golf event. Right after the Championship, we were playing it in upstate New York and I was running the match. When I arrived at the hotel, the phone rang. It was Tommy and he said, "Hey Joe, old buddy, let's have dinner."

Now I had just thrown him out of the game and its, "Joe old buddy, let's have dinner."

Tommy won seven of those matches while he was suspended and won $2,000 for each match - $14,000 while he was suspended. Then we had the appeal hearing and he was put on lifetime probation. He brought a lawyer to the hearing and that was the first time the PGA ever let a player bring an attorney to one of those hearings.

## Selling Television Rights

In 1962, it was quite apparent to the PGA and all of the players that television would play a huge part of the future of professional golf and create the vehicle to substantially increase purses. For years, the PGA, when contracting with the various sponsors, conveyed the television and radio rights to the sponsor to market as they saw fit. Most of the sponsors at that time were organizations that were using the tournament to promote their community as a great place to do business or as a great vacation destination. If they had the opportunity to sell the television or radio rights, their interest was the exposure they would receive from the broadcast rather than the amount of Rights Fees they would receive. Many of the sponsoring organizations were in the Junior Chamber of Commerce in their city. Their secondary interest was in raising funds for local charities.

At that time, most of the contracts with the sponsors were year to year. This provided the opportunity for the PGA to change its policy in regard to conveying the broadcast rights. It was felt that the PGA could retain the rights, package several tournaments together in an offering, and put the rights out to bid to the various television networks. A significant factor in all of this was the popularity of golf being created by the broad interest that Arnold Palmer was generating with his great play and the charisma he displayed with his fans.

To better understand how the television rights work, an explanation is in order. When a golfer joins the PGA and qualifies to play on the tour, a part of the requirement is that he will convey the use of his name and likeness to the PGA. The PGA then has the right to retain that use for its own purpose, or convey it to the sponsor for them to use as they see fit.

In 1962, it was decided that beginning in 1963, the television rights would be retained by the PGA. The sponsors were advised well in advance that this would be the case. It was explained to the sponsors that the purpose was to try to generate more rights fees, which would be used to increase the purses as well as to pay the operating costs of the tour. At that time, the players were paying an entry fee to compete in each tournament. The fee was $1.00 per every $1,000.00 of purse money, with a minimum of $100.00 per player per tournament. These operating expenses were the salaries of me and my staff, our travel expenses, and the administrative cost borne by the PGA Office.

When we arrived in Los Angeles for the first tournament of the year, the tournament sponsor, the Los Angeles Junior Chamber of Commerce, had not signed their contract. This was true of most of the other tournament sponsors. I talked to the Tournament Chairman about the contract and told him he would have to sign the agreement or we could not play the tournament. When we had not received the signed contract by Tuesday afternoon I told him we were cancelling the pro-amateur the next day because we could not play without a signed contract. They finally signed the contract and we played the Pro-Am as scheduled.

This same scenario continued for the next few tournaments with the contracts being signed prior to the playing of the pro-amateur. We finally decided that we would cancel any tournament where the contract was not signed by Sunday night at five-o'clock. We were playing in Palm Springs the week prior to the Phoenix Open and the Phoenix tournament sponsor, the Thunderbirds, had not signed their contract. I told Jack Tuthill, my assistant who was going to Phoenix early to do the advance preparation for the tournament, to tell the Thunderbirds we would cancel their tournament if Jack did not receive their signed contract by Sunday evening at five. The Thunderbirds had a meeting Sunday afternoon and came out of the meeting to tell Jack that they were not going to sign the contract. Jack called me and told me of the Thunderbirds decision. We announced the cancellation of the Phoenix Open to the golf media who were on hand for the final round of the Palm Springs tournament.

When Jack called to tell me of the Thunderbirds decision I told him to have all of the players in Phoenix to go to Tucson. Our thinking was that the Thunderbirds thought we would play without a contract. We wanted them to see a mass exodus of players out of town which would not set well with the business community, especially the hotel and restaurant businesses.

As soon as the cancellation was announced in Palm Springs, we began to receive calls from the Thunderbirds trying to get us to rescind the decision and play without an agreement. We told them we would not play without a contract. They requested a meeting in Phoenix on Monday which we agreed to with the understanding we could not meet before Monday evening. We agreed to meet at the Phoenix Country Club at nine on Monday evening. We did not want to meet prior to that because we wanted to have Marty Carmichael, our television attorney, present and he had to fly in from New York. We were sure that television was the reason they would not sign the contract.

When the meeting was convened, the Thunderbirds told us that they could not sign the contract because they had sold the rights for the 1963 and 1964 Phoenix Open to Dick Bailey's Sports Network, even though they did not own the rights. They had agreed to a fee of $5,000.00 per year for the rights. They were not too concerned about the amount of the rights fees. They were more concerned about being on television to showcase Phoenix as a winter resort destination. After a lot of discussion, we agreed to have the agreement with Sports Network conveyed to the PGA from the Thunderbirds, if this was agreeable to Dick Bailey. We called Dick who lived in Philadelphia and woke him up about 2 A.M. to discuss the situation and get his agreement. An agreement was drafted and signed as well as the tournament contract.

With the signing of the tournament agreement, my problems just began. We needed to get all of the players back to Phoenix for the Monday qualifying round to complete the field of players that would start play on Thursday, the first round of the tournament. The earliest we could conduct the qualifying was Wednesday. Thank goodness the qualifying was not scheduled for Phoenix Country Club because we had to play the pro-amateur there on Wednesday. The other problem was that the players had been released from their commitment to play at Phoenix when we cancelled the tournament. Fortunately, we had asked the players to stay on the West Coast while this problem played out. We knew where most of the players were. Most either stayed in Palm Springs or went into Los Angeles. Arnold Palmer flew his plane to El Paso and waited.

As it worked out, we were able to have the qualifying round Wednesday morning, play the pro-amateur at Phoenix Country Club, make the pairings for the first round of the tournament, and begin play Thursday morning on schedule. The only player who had committed but did not play was Art Wall. Art decided to go home for a week.

The end result of the PGA retaining the broadcast rights was that later that year we sold a ten tournament television package for $750,000.00. This started a major escalation of purses that has continued until today.

# Jack Nicklaus - Slow Play Penalty

Jack Nicklaus made his professional debut at the Los Angeles Open in January of 1962 after a huge amateur career. Jack had won the U.S. Amateur in 1959 and 1961, as well as almost winning the 1960 U.S Open. His start on the tour was highly anticipated with almost everyone believing he would be the next great star ultimately replacing Arnold Palmer. Unfortunately Jack got off to an inauspicious start. At Los Angeles, Jack tied for last place money and won $33.33. This was not what everyone expected and certainly did not reflect what was to come.

When Jack came on the tour, he had already developed a reputation as a very slow player. Slow play was a problem on the tour at that time as it is today. What most people don't understand is that there is no one who dislikes slow play more than the players themselves. At every meeting we had with the players this was a major subject of discussion, and the PGA Tour Tournament Committee constantly instructed me and my staff to pursue correcting the problem. The other thing about slow play on the tour is that the problem is caused by a handful of players. Most slow players think that they are not slow. Most slow players think that walking fast between shots makes up for the inordinate amount of time they spend in preparation for their shot. Jack had an additional problem of standing over the ball for a long time before taking his swing.

From the time Jack came on the tour, his slow play caused a problem. He would start his round and begin falling behind from the first hole. After five or six holes, he would be more than a hole behind. At that time slow play was defined as more than a hole behind your starting interval. This meant that a group would be about a hole and a half behind before they could be approached about their rate of play. They would be given a warning that they could be penalized if they did not get back in position in relation to the group in front of them.

This warning would bring on the excuses: "We had to spend time looking for a lost ball," "We are playing bad and this slows us down," "The greens are fast and we are three putting a lot," etc. It was always the other players' fault, the golf courses' fault, or the group in front was playing too fast. Jack and his group would then begin to play at a faster pace until they were no longer in jeopardy of being penalized. More than once, Jack would come to me and tell me that I had cost him two or three shots because I had given them a slow play warning. My response was always that I did not cost them any shots, that if they would keep their position on the course they would never see me.

Jack Niclaus penalized 2 strokes for slow play - Portland Open

As the year progressed, so did Jack's success. His first win came at the U.S. Open at Oakmont Country Club in Pittsburgh, Pennsylvania. Jack beat Arnold Palmer in an 18-hole playoff. This was a huge upset since Oakmont was a course that Arnold had played all of his life and he was the gallery favorite as a local boy. He was also the biggest super star on the tour.

Jack's next win came at the Greater Seattle Open in September. The following week we were playing the Portland Open at Columbia Edgewater Country Club in Portland, Oregon. Even though the tour would continue for another couple of months, this was going to be Jack's last tournament for the year.

The first round of the tournament Jack played well and was leading. He was playing extremely well having just won the Greater Seattle Open the prior week. His group, which was comprised of himself, Billy Casper, and Bruce Crampton, got out of position during the first round. I had to give them a slow play warning during the round. They had played the first round in the afternoon and were playing the second round in the morning. After a few holes, they had already fallen behind and I gave them a warning for their slow play.

They did not gain any ground in the next few holes so I spoke to them again at the tenth tee. They continued to play at a slow pace and it was obvious to me that Jack was the cause for the group falling behind. They continued to fall further behind on the back nine. I spoke to them for a third time on the 16th tee but it did not result in any improvement in their rate of play. This was the first time I had seen no effort by Jack to play faster after I had given him a slow play warning.

> In 1962, Jack Nicklaus was on his way to his second consecutive victory at the Portland Open Invitational when Tour official Joe Black walked into the scoring trailer. "Add two (strokes) to your card," Black told the young phenom.
>
> Nicklaus won the Portland event, and more importantly he learned a valuable lesson.
>
> "It was one of the best things that ever happened to me," Nicklaus recalled. "They wouldn't give you a slow-play penalty if you weren't slow."
>
> "Joe (Black) said you have to be ready to play when it's your turn," Nicklaus remembered. "When I first started, like a lot of kids, I would sit there and watch everybody else play and then when it was my turn to play then I'd start getting my yardage." *(Avid Golfer website, 6-10-2010)*

When they finished their round at the 18th hole, I met them when they walked off the green and told Jack I was penalizing him 2 strokes for slow play. His response was "where do I put it on the scorecard." I told him to add it to the 18th hole. Jack would have been leading the tournament by 2 strokes if it had not been for the penalty. As it was he was tied for the lead after the second round.

After Jack returned his scorecard, he was taken to the press room for an interview. I went to the press room and sat in the back of the room and listened to Jack's remarks. Just as he was finishing his interview I went to the locker room and waited for Jack at his locker. When Jack arrived at his locker I told him I thought it was time we talked about his slow play problem. I told Jack I could help him learn to be a faster player if he wanted my help.

He told me that he walked as fast as anyone getting to his ball. I told him that Don January and Julius Boros were two of the slowest players walking to the ball and two of the fastest players on the tour. Getting to the ball was not his problem. His problem came after he got to the ball. I also told him that the amount of time he stood over the ball was not his problem and did not bother me.

His problem was this: he was never prepared to hit his shot when it was his turn to play. I told him he was the first player to arrive at his ball in the fairway and on the green, but that he did not start stepping off his yardage, checking the wind direction, and selecting his club early enough. On the green he marked his ball and waited until it was his turn to putt before he started cleaning the line of his putt and reading the break of the green. I told him he should be doing all of these things prior to his turn to play and should have his club in his hand ready to hit his shot when it was his turn.

He told me he thought that would be rude. I told him to watch the other players and he would see that what I suggested was exactly what they were doing. After that conversation, I never had a problem with Jack the next two years that I ran the tour.

Incidentally, Jack won the tournament, his third win on the tour.

# Johnny Pott at the Ryder Cup

Johnny Pott had been playing the tour for a few years when he made his first of two Ryder Cup Teams. The first time was in 1963 with Arnold Palmer as the playing Captain. The matches were being played at East Lake Country Club, in Atlanta. East Lake was the home club of the great Bobby Jones.

The first professional at East Lake was George Sargent, who was the third President of the PGA of America. When he retired, he was succeeded by his son Harold Sargent, the 12th President of the PGA. It was Harold Sargent who convinced East Lake to host the matches.

Arnold Palmer was the playing captain in 1963, the last playing captain. After the matches, the PGA of America decided there were too many duties for the captain to impose those responsibilities on a player competing in the matches. The decision was made to select a non-playing captain. It was also decided the captain would be a player who had competed in the matches as well as having a significant stature in the game because of his playing record. It was thought that the player should have won a major championship and weight would be given to former winners of the PGA Championship.

When the team arrived at East Lake, Johnny Pott told Arnold Palmer that he wasn't playing too well and he wanted Arnold to know this so he could take it into consideration when making pairings for the matches. There were ten players on each team. Eight of the players on each team played each match with two players sitting out. There were two rounds of four matches each on the first two days. The first day was played in the foursome format. This is what we call alternate stroke play with each player playing every other shot. On the second day there were two rounds of four ball – better known in the United States as best ball play. On the third day there are eight singles matches in the morning and eight singles matches in the afternoon.

Each match was worth one point so there were 32 points available. The winning team had to had to win 16 ½ points to win the Ryder Cup.

During the practice round, Johnny Pott became more and more disappointed with his play and finally went to Palmer and told him to not play him until the singles matches. He did not want to be a burden to the team. Arnold's reply was that he would just pair with him because he could beat these "Jacks" by himself. Unfortunately, that was not the case. Palmer and Pott were beaten in the first round, 3 and 2, by Brian Huggett and George Will.

Arnold did not play Johnny again until the afternoon of the second round when they were ahead 8 ½ to 3 ½. He paired Johnny with Tony Lema, and they won one up over Peter Alliss and Bernard Hunt. He played him again in the morning singles where he lost to Brian Huggett three and one.

The matches in 1963 were not close as the American side won by a point count of 23 to 9. One aspect of the matches that is always enjoyable is the number of dignitaries from the game who attend. There are always former players, former captains, and past presidents of the PGA. One of those attending was Horton Smith who played on five Ryder Cup Teams and was named to four Ryder Cup Teams during World War II (even though the matches were not held). Horton was also the 10th President of the PGA of America.

At the conclusion of the matches, there is a Victory Dinner held for the two teams and the people who were part of the official party of the teams. I was invited to the Victory Dinner as the PGA Tour Director. I had been asked to conduct the play of the matches which involved making the course conform to the rules of golf, selecting the hole locations, setting the tee markers, and handling any rules questions that arose during the matches.

After the Victory Dinner at the Atlanta Athletic Club in downtown Atlanta, Horton Smith and I walked back to the hotel together and sat in the hotel lobby. I always enjoyed talking with Horton because he had such a magnificent career and had a great insight into the game. After we had visited for awhile, we decided to go to bed. I had to catch a flight to Las Vegas where we were playing the Sahara Invitational tournament the next week. Horton had to catch a flight to Detroit where he held the position of golf professional at the Detroit Golf Club.

When I got to Las Vegas and had settled into the hotel, I went out to the Sahara Country Club to see how things were going with preparations for the tournament. I had a message asking me to call PGA Headquarters. When I returned the call, I was told that Horton Smith had died of a heart attack after he returned home. It was a sad day for golf because Horton had done so much in the game. It was a sad day for me because Horton and I had become good friends. I have always been so thankful that I had the opportunity to spend time with Horton after the Ryder Cup Victory Dinner.

## Don January on the Lip of the Cup

The 1963 Phoenix Open was played at Arizona Country Club. On the final round, there was a great battle between Arnold Palmer, Gary Player, and Don January. The final hole at Arizona Country Club is a short par five that most of the players can reach with two shots. Don January was the first of the leaders scheduled to finish. When he reached the 18th hole, he knew he needed a birdie to have any chance of winning the tournament. Don missed the green with his second shot and pitched onto the green with a good chance of making a birdie.

Don hit his birdie putt and it looked like it was going in the hole. However, the ball stopped, overhanging the lip of the cup. Don walked around the hole, surveying the situation, and hoping the ball would drop into the cup. After a few moments he walked to a position where the sun was in a spot that when he took his hat off the shadow of the hat would fall on the ball. He was hoping the shadow would cause the grass to move causing the ball to drop. When this did not work, he told his fellow competitors that the ball was still moving and that if he putted the ball in the hole he would incur a two stroke penalty for playing a moving ball.

After a few minutes I got a call to come to the 18th hole. When I arrived, Don told me the ball was still moving and he did not want to play a moving ball because of the penalty he would incur. After looking at the ball, I told Don it did not look like the ball was moving and that I was declaring the ball at rest and relieving him of any penalty. He went ahead and holed his putt after a seven minute delay. A few minutes later Palmer and Player finished with Arnold winning the tournament and Player finished second, January finished third.

At the next Rules of Golf meeting this situation was reviewed and a rules change was made. The new rule provided that if a player's ball was overhanging the hole, the player has a reasonable amount of time to walk to the hole without undue delay and ten seconds to determine whether the ball is at rest. If by then the ball has not fallen into the hole it is deemed to be at rest. If it subsequently falls into the hole the player is deemed to have hold out with his last stroke and must add a penalty stroke to his score for the hole.

## Jerry Barber

Jerry Barber was a remarkable player. He was small in stature and had a very unique swing. He took the club outside the line on his back swing and rerouted it back inside. With that swing plane he typically hit a big slice. It really could not be called a fade; it was definitely a slice. If there were trees on the left side of the fairway he almost could not play the hole.

Jerry was also a notoriously slow player. With his slice and his small stature he was also one of the shortest hitters on the tour. To make up for his lack of length he was a remarkable short game player. He was a particularly good putter. Because of his slow play Jerry and I had several confrontations about his rate of play.

One year at the beginning of the tour, he suggested to the PGA Tournament Committee that my staff and I not be permitted to go onto the course unless we were called out to settle a rules question. He thought it was unfair for him and a couple of other players be "harassed" by our staff. He thought a player should be allowed to play at any pace that he wanted. He would not accept the fact that his slow play was affecting the play of most of the other players in the field.

Because Jerry was a short hitter, he was an advocate of increasing the number of clubs a player was permitted to use from 14 to 16 clubs. Every chance he got he would lobby me to approach the USGA Rules of Golf Committee to consider this change. He also tried to get the PGA Tournament Committee to advocate this change in the rules. Some members of the PGA Tournament Committee and I would meet with the USGA Rules of Golf Committee at the U.S. Open to discuss the rules and other aspects of tournament golf.

At the 1963 U.S. Open, played at The Country Club at Brookline, Massachusetts, we had one of these meetings. During the discussions about possible rules changes, the subject of increasing the number of clubs permitted was brought up. There had been several newspaper articles about the pros and cons of increasing the number of clubs. After much discussion in the meeting, Jay Hebert, one of the players on the PGA Tournament Committee, was given his opportunity to give his view on the subject. Jay's take was very simple: He said he thought the purpose of the game was to see who is the best player. If that is the case we should cut the number of clubs to seven, then we would find out who are really the best players.

That ended the discussion.

## Palmer on the Rocks

In the third round of the Bing Crosby National Pro-Amateur played at Pebble Beach Golf Links, Cypress Point Golf Club, and Monterrey Country Club, Arnold Palmer was playing at Pebble Beach on Saturday during the third round of the tournament. When Arnold came to the 17th hole, he was definitely in contention to win the tournament. However, that would change with one swing of the club. Arnold hit his tee shot over the green to the right. The ball bounded in front of the 18th tee, over the cliff, and down into the ocean to the right of the 18th hole.

Pebble Beach had a local rule providing that the ocean was played as a part of the course and not as a water hazard. At this particular time of the day, the tide was out so Arnold's ball came to rest in a rocky area below the cliff. Arnold looked over the cliff and saw his ball on the sand below and decided to go down to the beach and see if he could play the ball.

He made the determination that he thought he could play the ball and get it back up on the golf course. He then played a shot, but the ball hit the bank above the ball and bounced back down on the beach. This time the ball came to rest in some rocks where he could not get his club on the ball. Arnold then called for a rules official and I was handling the rules at Pebble Beach so I responded to the call.

Because the ocean was not being played as a water hazard, Arnold could not drop the ball back on the golf course under the water hazard rule. This meant that he either had to play the ball as it lay, or declare it unplayable and proceed under the unplayable ball rule. The unplayable ball rule provided that he had the option to drop the ball back at the place he played his previous shot from, drop within two club lengths from where the ball lay not nearer the hole, or keep the point where the ball lay between him and the hole and go back as far as he liked as long as he stayed on the course.

Because we were on national television at the time, Jimmy Demaret, who was one of the announcers handling the telecast for ABC, was dispatched to the 18th hole to cover the action.

By the time I arrived at the 18th tee to assess the problem, several people were there. Jimmy had climbed down the

bank to be closer to the action. Arnold and his caddie both were down on the beach, and three or four people who were out walking on the beach while the tide was out saw the crowd and wandered down to see what was going on. One of these onlookers was a man who was walking his dog, a beautiful Irish Setter.

When I told Arnold his options and mentioned keeping the point where the ball lay between him and the hole and going back as far as

"Palmer on the Rocks" one fo the most famous photos in golf history. Joe Black is seen in the white topcoat. (Used by permission from AP)

he liked, Demaret quipped that Arnold's nearest drop was Hawaii. However Arnold elected to drop the ball where he played from previously and try the shot again. He again hit the bank with his shot and bounded down into the rocks.

Because the ball had bounded more to the left when it hit the bank this time there was a large rock behind the ball.

Arnold wanted to know if he could try to drop the ball on the rock which would elevate the ball substantially off of the ground and make the shot much easier to get over the top of the cliff. I told Arnold that if he dropped the ball on the rock and it bounced off of the rock and nearer the hole or more than two club lengths from where the ball struck the rock when he dropped it, he would have to drop the ball again. If it again bounced nearer the hole or more than two club lengths, he would be required to place the ball at the spot where the ball struck the rock on the second drop.

Arnold decided to drop the ball on the rock because the rock was so tall he thought that if he dropped it the ball it would either bounce forward nearer the hole or would come to rest more than two club lengths from where the ball struck the rock. After he placed the ball on the rock he hit his shot. This time he was able to get the ball back on the golf course. By the time Arnold finished the hole, he had made a nine, which took him out of competition for the tournament.

By the time the third round was completed, people were talking about "Palmer on the rocks." Some of the photographs taken during the 30 minute drama are almost always in the golf publications when a tournament is played at Pebble Beach even forty years later. As an aside, I began to worry about getting Arnold extracted from his predicament because the tide had started to come back in and we would have to abandon our position.

## Billy Casper and Changing the Rules

The 1964 Carling World Open was played at Oakland Hills Country Club, which is located in Bloomfield Hills, Michigan. The tournament was sponsored by the Carling Brewery, a Canadian Beer Company. The company had been sponsoring a tournament in Canada and had aspirations of expanding the event to a major world status. They scheduled the event at Oakland Hills because of the stature of the club. They felt such a well-known venue would increase the prestige of the tournament. Their plan was to move the tournament around the world to all of the great venues.

At the tournament, Billy Casper did not anticipate that he would cause a change in the Rules of Golf because of an incident that happened on the first hole of the first round. Billy hit his tee shot into the right fairway bunker on the first hole. His caddie had moved down the right side of the fairway before the shot so he would have a better view of where his ball came to rest. When he saw the ball land in the fairway bunker, he walked down to the bunker before Billy arrived. He quickly noticed that one of the caddies from a previous group had neglected to rake the bunker. Noticing the damage left by the previous caddie, Billy's caddie took the rake and repaired the damage left in the bunker.

When he approached, Casper saw what his caddie was doing and yelled at him to stop, but it was too late. Casper knew that neither he nor his caddie was permitted to test the sand in the bunker prior to playing his shot. By raking the bunker his caddie was construed to have tested the sand. This called for a two stroke penalty.

When he finished the round, Billy contested the penalty, arguing that he gained no advantage by his caddie raking the bunker. His argument was that the players and their caddies were required to rake any damage to a bunker as a courtesy to players following behind. Why would a player want his caddie to rake bunkers if he faced a possible penalty for this action? The appeal was denied because the rule was very clear that such activity by a caddie called for the penalty.

However, Casper made a compelling argument, so I referred the situation to the USGA Rules of Golf Committee for review. At the next Rules of Golf Committee meeting, they reviewed the rule and changed it to provide that if a player gained no advantage from repairing damage away from his ball in a bunker there would be no penalty. Over the years there has been several rules changed because of similar incidents that occurred on the course during our tournaments.

## Cliff Roberts Letter

I resigned as PGA Tour Tournament Director at the end of 1964 to become Director of Golf at the 54-hole Brookhaven Country Club in Dallas, Texas. At the same time, I became Vice-President of Country Clubs, Inc. Brookhaven was the first golf club developed by Bob Dedman, the founder of Country Clubs, Inc. This company later became Club Corporation of America-- the first and most successful club development and management company in the world.

When I resigned from the tour, it created a fair amount of attention among the golf media. Because of this media attention, I received numerous letters from friends as well other people in the golf industry that I had come to know over the years.

One of those letters was from Cliff Roberts, the co-founder with Bobby Jones of Augusta National Golf Club. I had become well acquainted with Cliff from serving on the Masters Rules Committee for several years. Cliff congratulated me on my new position at Brookhaven and asked me to consider continuing to serve on the rules committee. He was kind enough to tell me I served a special purpose at Augusta and hoped I would continue to come as long as I liked. He also said he thought it would be in my best interest to continue to attend so I could maintain my many relationships developed over the years.

I followed his advice for 48 years.

# Ben Hogan, Ryder Cup Captain

The 1967 Ryder Cup Matches were played at Champions Golf Club in Houston. Champions is the great 36 hole golf club developed by Jimmy Demaret and Jackie Burke. Demaret won the Masters Tournament three times and was one of the great players of his era. Burke won the Masters Tournament as well as the PGA Championship. He also is the last player to win four consecutive tournaments on the tour.

This was one of the classic Ryder Cup Matches. The Captain for the British team was Dai Rees and for the American team it was the great Ben Hogan. Ben was one of the most prepared captains you will ever see. I was the chairman of the PGA Rules Committee and was in charge of conducting the play of the matches.

The rules of golf for match play are quite different from stroke play. Since all of the tournaments on the tour are played at stroke play, the players are not too familiar with match play rules. Consequently, Ben Hogan came to me and asked me if I would give the players a clinic

Ben Hogan addressing the 1967 Ryder Cup Team

regarding match play rules. We arranged to have the meeting in the locker room at Champions on Wednesday afternoon. He advised all of his team members about the clinic and asked them to plan to attend the meeting. All of the team members arrived except Arnold Palmer who was flying the British team over the course in his plane.

At the rules clinic, I walked the players thru the match play rules and answered all of the questions they raised. At the end of the clinic, I advised the players that because this was an international competition, they had the option of playing the 1.68" or the 1.62" diameter golf ball. At that time, the 1.62" ball was played in Great Britain and the 1.68" ball in the United States. Ben Hogan immediately said, "we will play the 1.62" ball."

Bobby Nichols, one of the American Team members, said he didn't want to play the 1.62" ball. Ben said then you won't play. Bobby decided it would be okay to play the 1.62" ball.

When Arnold arrived at the golf course on Thursday morning, he saw Ben Hogan who was very upset that Arnold had missed the rules meeting. Arnold told Ben that he did not think he wanted to play the 1.62" ball.

Ben said, "Arnold, I am not sure you are going to play at all."

The American team ended up playing the 1.68" ball and Arnold won all five of his matches. .

## Arnold Palmer at Brookhaven

When I went to Brookhaven, there was a big aviation industry golf tournament played there each year. It was sponsored by Southwest Aviation, a group of companies that worked together to restore and retrofit private aircraft. There were six hundred players that participated in the tournament.

Brookhaven had three golf courses, so we had a shotgun start in the morning on all three courses and again in the afternoon. Then we had a dinner for a thousand people in the evening. I had a planning meeting with their committee and we were talking about ways to enhance the tournament. I told them that it might be fun to honor a celebrity at the dinner. I said, "We might could get Arnold Palmer to come if we would honor him as the 'Flying Athlete of the Year.' If the date works he would probably come and accept the award."

So, I called Arnold and he told me he had an exhibition that Monday in Jackson, Mississippi, but said if we would send a Leer Jet over to pick him up he might come. At that time Arnold didn't have his own jet; he still had an Aero Commander.

Colonel Long was the distributor for Leer Jets in Dallas and he was a part of the Southwest Aviation group. So we told Arnold we would send a Leer to pick him up after his exhibition. Arnold asked if he could fly the Leer, and Colonel Long agreed. We sent a Leer to Jackson and picked up Arnold after his exhibition. We got permission from the FAA to let him buzz the golf course.

When he landed, Colonel Long picked him up in a Bentley and drove him to the club. This was in the days of go-go dancing. We had a go-go girl wrapped up in a parachute. We had him pull the parachute ripcord and the girl twirled out and started dancing and Arnold got in there and started go-go dancing with her. We had a ball that night.

The next year, we decided to honor Barry Goldwater as the "Flying Politician of the Year." I called Bob Goldwater, who was the founder of the Phoenix Open and a member of the PGA Advisory committee to get his assistance. Not only did Bob get Barry to come, but he also came as well, as did Barry Jr. who was a congressman from California. We set up a golf game with the three Goldwaters and Byron Nelson.

The next year we had Arthur Godfrey as the Flying Entertainer of the Year followed by Jimmy Demaret and Paul Hahn.

This proved to be a great way to enhance the tournament without the cost of paying a hefty appearance fee. All of

Arnold Palmer named "Flying Athlete of the Year"

these fellows loved flying and were thrilled to be recognized by the aviation industry.

## Arnold Palmer's Clubs

We played the Dallas Open at Oak Cliff where I was a member. If you know Arnold Palmer, you know he has always fiddled with his clubs. He did everything in the world with his golf clubs. He would rewind the grips during the practice rounds and be in the bag room beating on them with a hammer. He went into the bag room at Oak Cliff to tinker with his clubs and he saw my clubs in the bag room and started examining them. He couldn't keep his hands off of them. He came to me and said, "I've got to have your driver."

Arnold was with Wilson at that time and I was playing Wilson clubs. I had a driver that Joe Wolf, Wilson's tour representative, had made for me. He said "I've got to have it."

I said, "Arnold, you can't have that driver."

Then he said, "I've got to have that driver."

Again I told him no. Then he said, "Let me use it this week."

So he used it that week and drove great with it. He was supposed to put it back in my bag at the end of the tournament.

Well, Arnold, Gary Player, and I were going to Chicago the next week to film a television match between Gary and Arnold. Then Arnold said, "Why don't you fly up there with me on Monday? Since the match isn't until Friday we can mess around and play golf and go out to Wilson."

I told him no, that I had been gone from home all summer and I was going to stay home and would be in Chicago on Thursday. He said okay.

So I called him on Thursday when I got in and he said, "Hey, you've got to come over here and see your driver!"

I said, "What do you mean I have to see my driver?"

He said, "Well, I brought it with me and I took it out to Wilson and, boy, it's really great now!"

So I went over to his room and he had taken a wood rasp and rasped the toe right off my driver. He hooked everything so he did that to all his clubs. He had just destroyed my driver. I was really hot.

He went out the next day and drove it dreadfully. Then he tried to give it back to me. I said no, that he had ruined my driver and that he owed me. He asked me what I wanted and I said I wanted his back up putter. He had that famous putter that he made by welding a flange on the back of a Tommy Armour putter. He had two of them. He refused, saying he would be in trouble if he lost his putter.

Arnold Palmer using Joe's driver

We went to Seattle from there and every time I saw him I asked him about my putter? Next, we went to Portland for his last tournament, and every time I saw him I asked, "Arnie, where is my putter?"

At the end of the tournament I was standing near the scoreboard when he finished and he came over to me and said, "Come out here!"

I walked out into the parking lot and he pulled his irons out of his bag and handed them to me and said, "I don't want to hear another damn word from you about my putter!"

Those irons were the ones he used to win fourteen tournaments including the Masters, the British Open, and the Open – tournaments that enabled Arnold to set the all time money record of that time.

I still have them.

## Getting a Rules Official Out of the Shower

At the Masters Tournament the play is conducted by the Rules Committee. This committee consists of officials from various golf organizations. Some of these include the USGA, The R&A Golf Club of ST. Andrews, The PGA of America, The PGA Tour, The European Tour, and the LPGA, as well as other organizations from around the world. I served on the Rules Committee for 48 years. All of these officials contributed their time as volunteers.

There is a rules official assigned to each hole with the responsibility of handling any rules questions that may occur on his or her assigned hole. The Chairman of the Rules Committee, the Vice Chairmen, as well as a few of the more experienced officials were designated as "Rovers." They were assigned three or four holes to be available to assist in the event the official assigned to a hole was not sure of how a rule was to be interrupted. These officials were provided a golf cart so they could respond very quickly if needed.

Ike Grainger was a former President of the USGA as well as a former Chairman of the USGA Rules Committee. Ike was also a long time member at Augusta National Golf Club. Starting in 1968, my rules assignment was to serve the dual role as rules official at the 18th hole, as well as handling the scoring facility where we received the official scorecard from the players.

One year, Ike was assigned as the "Rover" for my hole. Late in the afternoon, Ike came by the scoring facility and told me that he would be available to assist me with any rules questions that came up on the 18th hole. That way I would not have to leave the scoring facility to run down the fairway to handle a rules question and leave the rules facility unattended. He said to just give him a call on his radio.

Doug Ford was playing in the last group. Doug is a former Masters champion. He was also a very fast, impatient player. On the last hole, Doug hit a sharp hook off of the tee that caught the trees on the left and dropped into a small stream. This stream was so far out of play that the officials marking the course prior to the tournament decided they did not need to designate it as a water hazard. When Doug found his ball in the stream he requested a rules official to determine how to play his next shot.

The request for a rules official was conveyed to me in the scoring facility. Since I had players in the scoring tent, I called Ike and asked him to handle the ruling with Doug. He responded that he was on his way and would be there in a few moments. The players finished checking their scorecards and left the facility.

In a few minutes I received another call telling me that Ike had not arrived to handle the ruling with Doug Ford. I called Ike again and asked him if I needed to handle the ruling, thinking that he may have gotten detained. Ike told me not to worry about it that he would arrive momentarily. Finally, Doug and his playing partners arrived in the scoring facility. Needless to say Doug was very upset that it had taken so long for a rules official to arrive. He also felt that the delay had caused his group to have to finish just before dark with difficult playing conditions.

The next morning at our rules committee meeting I asked Ike why it had taken him so long to respond to Doug Ford's request for a ruling. I told him Doug was very upset that it had taken so long to get there. Ike told me that he had a dinner engagement that evening and wanted to take a shower before going to dinner, so he went to his room to take a shower. He said he was in the shower when I called and had to finish and dress prior to being able to respond to my request to help Doug. He did not want to tell me over the radio he was in the shower.

## A Round of Golf with Ben Hogan

I have played golf with many great golfers, but only once with Ben Hogan. We made plans to enter the Dallas Open at Oak Cliff Country Club where Earl Stewart was the golf professional. Ben seldom played in tournaments any more, but Earl convinced Ben to play in the Dallas Open. However, he made it clear that he wasn't going to play in any practice rounds and wouldn't play in the pro-am the day before the tournament started. Ben had never played that course before but said he would like to.

So we put together a foursome of Earl, the Chairman of the Dallas Open, Ben, and myself, and played on the Saturday before the week of the tournament. As we approached each hole we told Ben about the hole and how to play it. We finally got to the 14th hole, which is a par 5 with a very narrow opening in the drive zone. We told Ben that a lot of people lay back short of this opening so they would have plenty of room to maneuver the ball through the opening. However if you put your drive down into this slot you can get the ball to the green in two.

Ben, Earl, and I decided to hit a driver to see if we could get our ball down into the slot. Earl and I had been out driving Ben by about 15-20 yards all day. Each hole had been a driving contest between Earl and me. When we arrived at the landing area for our drives, we noticed there was one ball about 10 yards in front of the other two balls. So, of course, Earl and I are both honing in on that front ball. As soon as we passed the first two balls, Ben said, "Wait a minute fellas, back here."

He had just zipped his ball right by us and knew it. He hit the ball on the green and made an eagle. He made 17 pars and one eagle that day. It was a lot of fun playing with him. He could really hit the ball. He was so crisp. I learned a lot from playing just one round with him that day.

## Palmer and the Bumblebee

For several years the Phoenix Open was played on alternating years at Phoenix Country Club and Arizona Country Club. One year when we were playing at Arizona Country Club I had one of my most unusual Rules of Golf questions. The Phoenix area had a pretty severe winter with a great deal of frost in the mornings. All of the golf courses in the Phoenix area usually overseed their greens with a rye grass because the normal Bermuda grass would go dormant due to the frost. Because of the severity of the frost, they did not get the normal germination of the rye grass. This caused the greens to have very sparse grass and be very bumpy.

The players were concerned about the condition of the greens. They were afraid that when they addressed the ball it would move which would result in a one stroke penalty. During the tournament I got a call that Arnold Palmer needed a ruling out on the course. When I arrived at the hole Arnold was playing, he told me that as he prepared to putt and after he had addressed the ball a bumblebee landed on his ball. When the bee flew off of the ball, the ball moved. Since, by definition the bumblebee was an outside agent he felt that an outside agent had moved his ball and, that even though he had addressed the ball, the penalty should not apply.

The discussion revolved around the question of whether a bee had the ability to move the ball because it did not seem to have the weight to cause a golf ball to move. However, because the greens were so bumpy it did not take much to cause a ball to move. There had been several cases of a player's ball moving after they had addressed it. After a lengthy discussion, I finally ruled that there was not a penalty involved because I could not conclusively prove that the bee could not move the ball. This brought in the premise that if there is not conclusive evidence the rule should be in favor of the player.

## Michigan Golf Classic

In 1968, the players on the tour decided to break away from the PGA of America, which had founded the PGA Tour and operated it from its inception. The players announced their decision to form a new tour during the middle of the year in 1968. This created all kinds of problems for the officers of the PGA and the sponsors of the existing tour tournaments. The PGA announced that if the players started their own organization, the PGA tour would continue. This created a real problem for both the players on the tour as well as the tour sponsors.

The decision to start a new tour was not unanimous with the players, and the sponsors did not know whether to align with the PGA, which had been the stabilizing entity of the tour, or to align with the players who had the star power to make their events successful. Jack Tuthill, the PGA Tour Tournament Director, had aligned himself with the players who were forming the new organization and was actively pursuing the tour sponsors and players to join the new organization. Max Elbin, the PGA President, and the other PGA officers felt Tuthill was violating his responsibility to the PGA. They had a real problem. If they fired Tuthill, they did not have anyone else on the tour staff who could garner the confidence to take his place. Moreover, they did not know where the other staff members' loyalties were.

I had resigned at the end of the 1964 tour season as the PGA Tour Tournament Director to become the Director of Golf at Brookhaven Country Club in Dallas, and to become Vice President of Golf for Club Corporation of America. When I left the tour, I recommended Jack Tuthill, who was my assistant, to replace me.

Max Elbin and the PGA officers approached me to see if I would take a temporary leave of absence from Brookhaven to come back and run the tour during this crisis. After discussing it with Vic Rimes, the club manager at Brookhaven, and Bob Dedman, the Owner of CCA, I agreed to go back and run the tour while these problems were being solved.

I flew to Washington D.C. to meet with Max Elbin, who was also the Golf Professional at The Burning Tree Golf Club in Bethesda, Maryland. After meeting with Max to get a briefing on the situation and discuss strategy, I went to Boston where the tour event was being played, to assume my new duties. I had a meeting with Jack Tuthill to tell him that I had been asked to assume the operation of the tour. Jack tendered his resignation at that meeting. I began immediately to meet with the players and sponsors to determine their loyalties.

The sponsors had formed an organization called the American Golf Sponsors Association. They decided to hold a meeting in Houston, to give both organizations an opportunity to present their future plans. They would then discuss the situation and decide which organization they were going to join. After giving the PGA and the new players' organization the opportunity to meet with them, they went into a closed session to make their decision. When they came out of the meeting they held a press conference and said "we have decided to go with the dancing girls." This meant that the PGA had to start finding new sponsors for a new tour to be run by the PGA of America. Max asked me to begin to find sponsors.

As you can imagine there was a tremendous amount of media attention given to this whole situation. It was well-documented that the PGA was looking for sponsors for a new tour. At the same time, the political situation within the PGA was changing. President Max Elbin was reaching the end of his term of office and Leo Fraser, the Secretary of the PGA, was scheduled to move up and become the new

President of the PGA. Max had taken a very hard line with the players, advocating that if they did not like the way the tour was being run they could leave. Leo was bringing a new strategy of reaching out to the players and seeing if the differences could be resolved.

I began to reach out to groups that had expressed an interest in sponsoring an event on the PGA Tour. The first event I booked was The Sunol Golf Classic, to be played at the Sunol Golf Club in Sunol, California. Sunol was a community just outside of Oakland. This event was to be played the first week in January, the same date the Los Angeles Open was scheduled to be played on the new tour. The idea was to create a conflict of interest between the two events so the players would have to choose which event to play. The PGA Tour had a rule that if a player played in an event in conflict with a tour scheduled event they would be suspended from the tour.

The second event I scheduled was The Michigan Golf Classic, to be played at Shenandoah Golf Club in Detroit. This tournament was scheduled for the summer. Lou Powers, the President of the Michigan Section of the PGA, asked me to speak to the owner of Shenandoah Golf Club who had contacted him about sponsoring a tournament to promote his club. I asked Lou about the financial strength of Shenandoah Golf Club and the owner of the club. Lou did not know but said the owner would be willing to escrow the purse so there would be no risk to the purse being paid.

When Leo Fraser was elected President of the PGA, he reached out to Gardner Dickinson and Dan Sikes who were heading up the players effort to start a new tour. After intense negotiations between the PGA and the players group, the decision was made to form a new division of the PGA to be called the PGA Tour Tournament Division. The Tournament Division would be governed by a Policy Board comprised of four players, the three officers of the PGA of America, and three independent business men. The policy board would be chaired by one of the independent directors, with the President of the PGA as the vice-chairman. This Board would be autonomous. The day-to-day operation of the tour would fall to a Commissioner selected by the board. Much to everyone's surprise, Joe Dey, the long time Executive Director of the United States Golf Association, agreed to become the first Commissioner of the PGA Tour.

I had been told by Leo Frazier when he was elected President of the PGA, to stop trying to schedule tournaments for a new tour. He felt confident that a resolution could be found. A part of the settlement agreement with the players provided that any tournaments that I had scheduled would be honored. Joe Dey and the tour staff would make every effort to provide both tournaments with a good field.

As soon as Joe Dey was named commissioner of the tour, I called him and asked him if he wanted me to brief him on the terms of the two tournaments I had scheduled. He told me it would not be necessary because he was developing a new sponsor's agreement and any tournament that did not sign the new agreement would be dropped. That completed my responsibilities to the PGA, so I returned to my position at Brookhaven. This was in December of 1968.

The Sunol tournament was played without any problems and the tour returned to business as usual. At the completion of the Michigan Golf Classic, the sponsor told the PGA Tour staff that they did not have the money to pay the purse, so they were going to have to default. They claimed that because there were two tournaments scheduled that week the tour had not provided them with a representative field. As a result, they did not get the sponsor and gallery support they needed to be successful.

When I read in the paper on Monday morning that the Michigan Golf Classic had defaulted on their purse, I called Joe Dey to find out what had happened. When I asked him if he did not require the sponsor to escrow the purse as I had required them to do in order to get on the schedule, the phone went silent. Finally, Joe asked me why I had not told him of this requirement. I reminded him that I had called him and offered to meet with him to discuss the terms of the agreements with Sunol and The Michigan Golf Classic.

Larry Ziegler won the tournament which was his first win on the tour. The total purse was supposed to be $100,000 with the winner getting $20,000 plus a new car. However, for the tournament the purse paid was $50,000 and Larry won $9,000. Later in the year the PGA Tour and The PGA of America split the responsibility and paid the purse.

## All Star Golf Las Vegas

In 1969 there was a made-for-television golf series called All Star Golf, which was produced by Peter DeMet Productions. The format of the program called for the winner of each match to continue playing matches until he lost. The winner of each match received two thousand dollars and the loser received one thousand dollars. For the most part, the matches were scheduled on Monday and Tuesday so they would not conflict with the regular tour tournaments.

Peter DeMet Productions contracted with me and Jack Tuthill, my assistant, to conduct the matches. Our job was to mark the course so we could more easily play under the Rules of Golf. We would set the hole placements and the tee markers, and we also handled any rules situations that arose during the match.

A match was scheduled for the Desert Inn Country Club, located at the Desert Inn Hotel in Las Vegas, Nevada. In those days, many of the original hotels in Las Vegas were built and owned or controlled by people reputed to have connections with the mafia. The people who built the Desert Inn were all from Cleveland and were allegedly involved with the Cleveland mafia - Morris Kleinman, Allard Roen, Moe Dalitz, and Papa Walsh.

Because of our schedules, I asked Jack Tuthill to conduct the play at the Desert Inn. We would usually arrive the day before the match was scheduled in order to prepare the golf course. For this match, everyone was staying at the Desert Inn Hotel. In order to access the golf course, the villas, and the golf shop, you had to pass through the lobby.

Jack Tuthill and his wife Dorothy were former FBI Agents. They knew the identity of most of the key mafia people. As they were sitting in the hotel lobby on Monday evening before one of the matches, they noticed a group of people that they recognized as members of one of the mafia families pass through the lobby. In a few minutes, another group from another family also walked through the lobby.

A little while later, one of the TV production crew members came up to Jack and Dorothy and told them they had made a reservation for them to attend the dinner show at the Stardust Hotel and that a car was waiting outside to take them. He also provided two hundred dollars to pay for the show.

Jack and Dorothy had a great time at the show and even spent a few minutes in the casino. When they returned to the Desert Inn, there were no mafia people in sight. Obviously the mafia kept track of FBI agents and someone had recognized them. Jack did not know if the mafia knew they were no longer with the FBI. Jack heard later that the mafia was having a meeting in Las Vegas at that same time.

## Significant Events in Golf 1960-1969

**Television:** The growth of tournament golf in the 1960's was huge. There were many factors that contributed to this explosion. Without a doubt the most important factor was the proliferation of television golf. There had been some televised golf tournaments for several years with the first being a local telecast of the U.S. Open in 1947 at St. Louis Country Club, St. Louis, Missouri. The first nationally broadcast event was the Tam O'Shanter World Championship from Chicago in 1953.

There were some TV broadcasts through the last half of the 1950's, but the explosion was driven by Arnold Palmer and his exploits when the cameras were turned on. This was enhanced when Jack Nicklaus and Gary Player joined the tour and the competition between the "Big Three of Golf" became so intense. Also important was when the PGA of America decided to retain the broadcast rights to all of the PGA Tour tournaments in 1964. Previously the rights had been given to the individual tournaments. This gave the PGA the ability to package all of the tournament TV rights and create a bidding process available to all interested TV broadcast entities. The rights fees paid by the TV networks increased tenfold and these increases in fees were used to subsidize the purses of the tournaments. With the larger purses there was much more interest from the TV viewing public which expanded the interest in the game.

**Communications:** During the 1960's there were a couple of inventions which dramatically improved the way tournaments were conducted. In the early 1960's, Motorola developed a small hand held two way radio. The ability to develop a communications system with these radios completely changed the way we operated golf tournaments.

These radios were very expensive when they were first brought to market. Neither the PGA nor the tournament sponsor could afford the expense of buying enough to set up a communication system for a tournament. However the PGA was able to convince Motorola there was value to having our staff using the radios each week at the tour tournaments. We agreed to place a notice on the scoreboard that PGA communications was furnished by Motorola. The radios had interchangeable batteries so we could use them all day simply by changing batteries when the need required.

**Spray Paint:** When we arrived at a tournament site one of our first responsibilities was to mark the golf course so the tournament could be played by the rules of golf. This entailed marking the water hazards so the margin of the hazard could be determined and whether the hazard was a regular water hazard or a lateral water hazard. This was done by painting small stakes, red to define the lateral water hazards and yellow to define the regular water hazards. We also had to define the ground under repair on the course. This was done by white lime that was normally used to mark the lines on baseball and football fields.

If we had a lot of water hazards on the course we would have to paint several hundred stakes and pound them in the ground around the edge of the creeks and lakes on the course. We would have to use a spreader made especially for this purpose to mark the lines around the ground under repair. The problem with using lime was when it rained the lime would be washed out and we would have to mark the ground again. As you can imagine it was a lot of work to get the course prepared for tournament play.

In the early 1960's, a small company in Fox Valley, Illinois, Fox Valley Marking Systems, developed a paint that was packaged in a spray can. It was produced in many colors including white, red and yellow. They also developed a spray gun that you could attach to the can and walk upright, spraying the paint. This dramatically reduced the cost and time required to mark a golf course. There was also the benefit that the paint would not wash away with rain. This was a huge benefit in the management of a golf tournament and as such was one of the significant inventions that benefited golf in the 1960's. Eventually every golf course in the country was using the Fox Valley Marking System to mark their course for everyday play.

**World Wide Endorsements:** In the late 1950's and early 1960's when a player on the tour signed an endorsement agreement with any manufacturer it usually only applied to the United States. The primary reason for this was that the golf manufacturers had not developed worldwide distribution systems. The few who did have a worldwide presence usually manufactured a different style of club overseas than was manufactured in the U.S. When IMG and other managers of players began to maximize the income of the players they represented, they looked overseas for business opportunities. One of the first opportunities was for the American players to endorse products in foreign companies. Some of the opportunities were with American companies while others were with foreign manufacturers.

Some of these endorsement deals required the players to play exhibitions or play in tournaments in other parts of the world. Usually, if a player made these appearances he was paid an appearance fee. This was in addition to any money he would win in any tournament he played. It was not unusual for a player to have to play equipment or wear clothing from a different manufacturer in these foreign appearances, or to have one set of clubs for the U.S., another set for Britain, a third set for Australia, and another set for Japan. As golf became more popular around the world the American manufactures began to open up distribution systems around the world which led to player contracts that required the player to use their equipment worldwide.

**Roping Fairways Tee to Green:** When I started playing the tour in 1955 the tournaments roped around the tees and green to control the gallery. Some of the leading groups had gallery marshals assigned to their groups with a long rope which they stretched across the fairway behind the players to control the gallery. I believe the Masters Tournament was the first tournament to place ropes completely around each hole. This was a great improvement for tournament administration. As galleries increased in size it would have been impossible to conduct the play of a tournament without this gallery control system.

**Leaderboards and Walking Scorers:** As the Motorola hand held radios became more affordable, the tournaments were able to develop a communications system. With this came leader boards. The first tournament to use leader boards was the Masters Tournament. The tournament sponsor erected large scoreboards around the course and displayed the names of the leading players in the tournament on the board. The sponsor of the tournament would get volunteers to walk with the players carrying a two way radio. The walking scorers would call in the scores at the end of each hole. These scores would then be placed on the leader boards which gave the gallery around the course the opportunity to keep up with the play of all the leading players. This system also gave the players the opportunity to monitor the play of their competitors.

**Tournament Players Split with the PGA of America:** One of my stories dealt with the split between the tournament players and the PGA of America. The end results was the formation of the PGA Tour Tournament Players Division and ultimately the PGA Tour as a separate organization. With this split came the appointment of Joe Dey the Executive Director of the United States Golf Association as the first Commissioner of the PGA Tour. This was one of the most significant events to occur in the 1960's and probably in all of golf.

**Travel:** The travel arrangements during the early years of the tour have been well documented. The early mode of travel was either by automobile or train. If the players elected to travel by automobile they usually traveled two or three to the car and shared the expenses. With the purses being offered at the time this type of travel was almost a necessity for all but the very top players. Trains were the preferred mode of travel by some players, especially before the tour developed into a schedule of weekly tournaments.

As air travel became more wide spread and affordable, some of the leading players began to fly commercially between tournaments. This helped the players with their physical stamina and created the opportunity to take advantage of other financial ventures between tournaments. It became very popular for the players to play exhibitions on Monday or Tuesday between tournaments. Charitable organizations began to schedule one or two day Pro-Amateur events between tournaments and guaranteed the players a minimum fee with a purse which gave the players the opportunity to win significantly more money.

Johnny Bulla was the first professional to fly his own plane. He had been a Commercial Airline Pilot and bought a DC 3 to travel between tournaments. He charged other players a fee to fly with him to offset his cost of operating the plane. Arnold Palmer was the first modern day player to own and fly his own plane. Arguably, you could say it was Arnold that showed everyone the benefit of using a plane to conduct his business on the tour. Soon, more and more players were flying their own planes. Most of the ones not flying their own planes was flying commercially. This ultimately led to players leasing time on planes. All players use some form of air travel today.

**Del Webb:** Real estate developer and part owner of the New York Yankees Baseball Team, Del Webb developed the concept of building golf oriented retirement communities. Webb completed his first development, which he named Sun City, just west of Phoenix. He effectively sold a retirement lifestyle in a planned community that provided every amenity that a retiree could want or need. This included several golf courses, community centers where various arts and crafts were taught, concerts provided by leading entertainers, and various other sports venues such as croquet courts. The community also had its own health care facilities. Sun City was a master planned city that accommodates several thousand citizens with every type of planned activity a retiree could want.

**The Caucasian Clause in the PGA Constitution:** Until the mid 1960's, the PGA Constitution had a provision that in order to become a member the person had to be Caucasian. This became a huge issue because of the civil rights movement and the development of several black golfers who wished to play the PGA Tour. The PGA membership voted to eliminate this clause which opened the door for such black players as Charlie Sifford, Calvin Peete, Jim Thorpe, Jim Dent, Lee Elder, and many others to gain access to the PGA Tour. All of these players and several others won tournaments on the tour. Charlie Sifford was the first black player elected to the World Golf Hall of Fame and Peete played on the 1985 Ryder Cup Team. Lee Elder was the first black player to play in the Masters Tournament. The removal of the Caucasian clause was long overdue.

**Club Professional Championship:** One of the issues between the PGA of America and the tour players that brought about the split in 1968 was the number of club professional in the PGA Championship as well as the number in the regular tour tournaments. The tour players felt the club professionals were not competitive in these type events. For this reason they felt players who were playing the tour for a livelihood were being deprived of the opportunity to make a living. The statistics bore this out. The PGA felt these events were owned by the PGA and they had the right to determine who played in the tournaments. The club professionals wanted to be able to play with the tour players and wanted their members to see them compete in these events.

Leo Fraser, the President of the PGA came up with a solution to the problem. He suggested the PGA start a new tournament which would be called The Club Professional

Championship. The club professionals from around the country would qualify to play in this event and their performance in the event would qualify them for the PGA Championship. This tournament is now called The PGA National Professional Championship.

**International Golf:** Even though players from other parts of the world would come to the United States to play in a few events prior to the 1960's, this decade was the true start of international golf. With the purses increasing, television exposure, and American players beginning to travel overseas to compete, it created a new level of awareness and interest for the international players. The international players wanted to compete against the best in the world and the PGA tour was the opportunity to achieve this goal. Some of the premier players to come to the U.S. during this decade were Gary Player, Peter Thomson, Bruce Crampton, Tony Jacklin, Stan Leonard, Al Balding, Bob Charles, Roberto De Vicenzo and Bruce Devlin.

**Jack Nicklaus** joined the PGA tour and became the greatest player of all time.

Joe Black with legendary golfer
and entertainer - Bob Hope

Jack Nicklaus and Byron Nelson

Joe with Sam Snead at the Oak Cliff Country Club in Dallas

# Decade of the 70's

## PGA-USGA Rules Workshops

One of the biggest problems with administering major golf tournaments such as the U.S. Open, the PGA Championship, the Masters Tournament, and the Ryder Cup Matches, are the people qualified to serve as Rules Officials. I started working on the PGA Tour in January of 1958. One of my primary responsibilities was the handling of the day to day rules situations that arose during the playing of the tournaments each week.

When I first started on the tour, I probably did not realize the importance of that part of the job, or how ill prepared I was to do the job. On my first day of the Los Angeles Open I had to handle thirty six rules situations. When the day was over, I told Harvey Raynor, the Tournament Director, that I was not sure I could handle the job. Knowing that it was just one of the next several years of managing golf tournaments, I vowed to become one of the best rules officials in the world. Learning the rules is not rocket science. It requires studying the Rule Book and rules Decision Book, and more importantly handling rules situations under fire when you have to be right each time. There is no margin for error.

As time went on, I decided to train more people to become interested in the rules, with the idea that some of them would like to make this a career path, either as a volunteer for local, state, or national golf events, or as a professional. I started by offering my services as a speaker at PGA of America educational seminars on a local, sectional, and national level. I began traveling all over the country, speaking at these seminars, challenging the golf professional in attendance to take a greater interest in the rules. As time went on, I began to see some fruit of my labor. I was able to recommend some of these professionals to serve on the PGA Rules Committee.

After I joined the USGA Rules Committee as a consulting member, I put forth an idea to the Rules of Golf Committee. The thought was to develop a joint program, sponsored by the USGA and the PGA of America, to conduct week-long rules seminars each year that would culminate with a test. It was one hundred questions in length and covered all of the rules as well as the definitions in the rule book.

An individual would have to make a score of 92 in order to become a Certified Rules Official. The PGA and the USGA would only invite Certified Rules Officials to serve on their Rules Committees and to help conduct the play of their various championships. The Rules Committee voted to recommend the program to the USGA Executive Committee for adoption. The USGA Executive Committee concurred and the PGA-USGA Joint Rules Seminars were born. They have been a huge success with hundreds of golfers each year attending the seminars.

## Ducks in the Pond

The 1970 PGA Club Professional Championship was played at Sunol Valley Country Club, in California. Sunol is a small community just outside of Oakland. This country club is a 36-hole facility, with a clubhouse sitting on a hill overlooking the 18th hole on the two courses. There is a lake separating the two final greens, which had become the habitat of some ducks.

The ducks were a great favorite of some of the members, as well as with the staff. There was young lady on staff at the golf shop who was particularly fond of the ducks. When I made a trip to Sunol a few months prior to the tournament, I told the Golf Course Superintendent that he should plan to pen the ducks during the tournament. They would obviously be very disruptive to the players and gallery as well as the mess they would leave behind when they were on the greens could create real problems. The young lady in the golf shop thought I was just terrible to make such a request.

When I returned for the tournament, the ducks had been penned up as I had requested. However, the lady in the golf shop complained to me each time I came to the golf shop about how cruel I was being to the ducks by keeping them penned up for so long.

Each day prior to play, I would go around the course to make sure all of the hole locations were correct and to make sure the course was ready for play. On Sunday morning when I arrived at the 18th hole, there was a wooden duck floating on the lake, which had been painted black with the name

Joe chasing ducks from the pond - 1970 PGA Championship, Sunol Valley Country Club

Joe printed on the side of the duck. When I looked up to the golf shop, all of the golf staff were having a big laugh at my expense.

I removed the wooden duck from the lake and took it up to the golf shop to return it to the lady who had placed it in the lake. She asked me to keep it as a memento of the tournament. She just wanted to see if I would remove it from the lake as well.

# Golf Ball Size

When the decision was made by the USGA and The Royal and Ancient Golf Club of St. Andrews to unify their rules, one of the more difficult issues concerned the size of the golf ball. The ball size allowed by the R&A was 1.62" in diameter while the USGA permitted size was 1.68". If there was an international competition the players had the option of playing either ball.

The effort to develop the uniform code took place over several years with the Rules of Golf committee from both organizations holding their own meetings to develop their positions on the various changes. There was a joint committee of both organizations which met during the U.S. Open, the British Open, and the Masters Tournament to present the positions of each organization and either accept one position or the other or to find a common ground. After the joint meetings, the committees of each organization would meet again to get a report on the results of the joint meeting and to determine how to move forward in preparation for the next meeting.

When all of the issues were resolved except the ball size, the debate began. The R&A argument revolved around the playing conditions in Britain and Ireland which tended to be very windy. They felt these conditions supported the smaller ball because it could be controlled better in windy conditions. The USGA position was that the smaller ball would bury in the bunkers with our softer sand. We also felt that when the smaller ball was hit into our long rough it would tend to bury deeper and be much more difficult to extract. There was not much progress being made toward a solution so a suggestion was made to consider developing a 1.66 inch diameter ball as a compromise.

The R&A were able to get the Dunlop Golf Company to make some 1.66" diameter balls for the two Rules Committees to try. Each of us was sent one dozen of the new balls to try. Not only did I try the ball, but I gave some of them to my members at Brookhaven. When all of the reports were in, I did not receive a very favorable review from my members and I did not like the way the ball played either. When results came into the two rules committees, it was obvious the compromise ball was not going to be the answer to our ball size problem. There was also a real concern that if the 1.66" diameter ball was adopted that there would be litigation from the golf ball manufacturers because of the huge cost that they would incur to retool their process to bring the new ball to market.

I also told the British PGA what I had told the USGA Rules Committee. I felt that they would not be successful in the Ryder Cup Matches nor would their players be successful on the American tour until they switched to the 1.68" diameter ball. Their ball was too forgiving in the wind and buried easier in the roughs and in our soft bunker sand. The British PGA decided to start using the 1.68" diameter ball in their competitions and the American tour players would not embrace the 1.66" diameter ball so that started the demise of the 1.62" diameter ball.

The biggest mistake we all made is that we did not keep any of the 1.66" balls. They would be highly sought after by golf ball collectors. When I tell my collector friends about the ball they were not even aware that it had been produced.

## No Bare Feet in the Park

The 1971 PGA Championship was played at PGA National Golf Club in Palm Beach Gardens, Florida. I was the Chairman of the PGA Rules Committee and as such conducted the play of the Championship. Part of my responsibility was to coordinate with all of the local committees to be sure they were operating as they should. Because we were playing at PGA National, our own club, we named one of the members of the PGA Board of Directors to serve as Chairman of the various committees.

Jay McClure, our board member from Texas, was appointed Chairman of the Caddie Committee. We had decided to require all of the caddies to wear tennis shoes while on the golf course. The greens were soft and as a result were marked up from all of the golf shoes on the greens. Since most of the caddies wore golf shoes, we felt that if we could eliminate them walking on the greens with spikes we could eliminate half of the spike marks. We also thought there could be an added benefit from the caddies wearing tennis shoes. Perhaps the tennis shoes would flatten some of the spike marks being created by the players.

We bought enough tennis shoes to provide a pair for each caddie. The manufacturer sent extra shoes so we would be able to fit all of the caddies with their proper size. Jay set up a changing area in the caddie room to pass out the shoes to the caddies. After a couple of days he had supplied all of the caddies with their shoes.

After we began play on Thursday with the first round of the tournament, I received a call from one of the Rules Officials on the course that one of the caddies was bare footed. I drove over to the hole where the group was playing and sure enough there was a bare footed caddie. After the completion of the hole I asked the caddie why he was not wearing the shoes we had given him. He said he wore a size 14EE shoe and we only had a size 12D. He said the shoes hurt his feet so bad that he quit wearing them. I called Jay and told him of the situation and that he needed to get his caddie some shoes.

Jay went to the golf shop to try to find a solution to his problem. They did not have a pair of larger tennis shoes but they did have a pair of size 14D golf shoes. Jay bought the shoes and removed the spikes. He then took them out to the caddie and had him put on the shoes. Jay called me on the radio and said, "Mr. Chairman I want to report to you that there are no bare feet in the park."

# Bob Dedman and the Out of Bounds Rule

Efrem Zimbrelist,Jr. was the star of the TV show, "The F.B.I." in the late 1960's and early 1970's. He was in Dallas on business and was invited by Bob Dedman to join him for a round of golf at Brookhaven. Bob was the founder of Club Corp which operated more golf clubs around the world than any other company.

It was in the spring of 1972 and we had our normal spring winds, which were out of the south at 15-20 mph. When Bob called to tell me they were planning to play, I asked him if it would be ok to start them on the 10th hole of our Masters Course. We had people scheduled to play off of the first hole and this would not interrupt their game.

When they arrived at the golf shop, I accompanied then to the 10th tee to get them started. Our 10th hole was a short par four of 350 yards, but it had a roadway on the left and out of bounds on the right side of the hole. The hole played from the east to the west, so the south wind was blowing across the hole from the left.

Bob was noticeably nervous as he prepared to hit his first shot. The south wind took the ball and blew it out of bounds on the right side of the hole. He hit another shot which also blew out of bounds as did his third and fourth shots. Obviously Bob was embarrassed and upset. He finally hit the ball in the fairway and they went on with their round. I did not think too much of the incident and went on about my business.

A couple of days later I got a call from Bob asking me to come over to his office, he had something he would like to discuss with me. When I arrived, he brought up the incident on the 10th hole. He told me he thought that we should change the rule to play the out of bounds the same as a lateral water hazard. This meant that if a player hit a ball out of bounds he would go down to where the ball went out of bounds and drop the ball with a one stroke penalty.

I told Bob we could not do that because it would violate the rules of golf. He said he did not care, that he wanted me to implement the change at all of our clubs immediately. I told him I could not do that because the USGA would not honor the handicaps of our members in any of their competitions. Furthermore, the USGA would suggest to the state and local golf organizations to do the same thing. Bob was not aware of the ramifications of such a change, so he finally agreed we should not make our own rule for out of bounds.

I could tell Bob was not going to let the subject die. He continued to bring it up to me. He wanted to know if I would appeal to the USGA to change the rule. I told him I would not approach the Rules Committee to change the rule because I thought it was correct. He then asked me if I could arrange for him to meet with the Rules Committee to try to convince them to change the rule. I told him the Rules Committee had a policy of not meeting with individuals during their meetings. He continued to ask me to arrange a meeting. I finally agreed to call the chairman of the committee and prevail upon him to let Bob attend the Rules Committee during the U.S. Open at Pebble Beach.

I made the call and to my surprise the USGA agreed to let Bob address the meeting at Pebble Beach. Bob then started lobbying me to go with him when he spoke to the committee. I told him I simply did not agree with what he was trying to do so I would not feel comfortable attending the meeting.

Bob made the trip to Pebble Beach but was unsuccessful in convincing the USGA to change the rule. Bob did make history by being the first non-member to be permitted to attend a Rule Committee meeting. When he returned from Pebble Beach he never brought up the subject again.

## Paul Runyan at Tanglewood

The 1974 PGA Championship was played at Tanglewood Country Club in Clemmons, North Carolina. This was a golf course developed by Reynolds Tobacco Co. It proved to be a pretty good test of golf for the best players in the world. Lee Trevino beat Jack Nicklaus by one shot for the victory.

In the PGA Championship, all former winners are eligible to play in the tournament. Another unique feature of the Championship is the fact that all players that complete 36 holes of play receive a check, just for competing. There is a past champions dinner on Tuesday night, a fun affair that all of the past champions enjoy attending. Because they get a check if they play the first two rounds of the tournament, most of the past champions play even though they are no longer competitive. This gives them the opportunity to come to the Championship and attend the past champions dinner and pay their expenses with the money won for completing the first two rounds of play.

Paul Runyan was one of the past champions playing at Tanglewood. He was a two time winner but won his last championship in 1938, thirty-six years earlier. After Paul played a practice round on Tuesday before the tournament, he came to me with a question and a suggestion. The 10th hole was a long par four that required about a 200 yard carry over a lake to reach the fairway. Paul asked me if I planned to use the back tee for the first two rounds. When I told him I did, he said that he could not hit the ball far enough in the air to carry the ball over the lake. I told him that I could not set the course up to accommodate the shortest hitter in the field. Paul was not happy with my answer and told me he probably would not be able to complete the first round.

After he finished the first round Paul, who had shot an 84 for the round, withdrew from the tournament. Curious about his score on the 10th hole, I stopped by the scoreboard to check his scorecard. To my amusement one of the few pars on his scorecard was a four at the 10th hole.

In 1979, at the PGA Championship at Oakland Hills Country Club in Birmingham, Michigan, we changed our policy regarding the need for a past champion to complete the first 36 holes of play in order to receive last place money if they missed the cut. We decided to pay all past champions an amount of money equal to the amount paid to all players who did not make the cut. This was well received by many of the past champions who really did not want to play in the tournament but did want to come to the past champions dinner and have an opportunity to play the course during the practice rounds.

## Tony Lema and Tony Bennett

I had a call from Tony Lema one spring Sunday afternoon telling me that Tony Bennett was in Dallas for an engagement and had called wanting to play a round of golf. Tony knew that Sunday was a very busy day for member play at the club, but he wanted to accommodate Tony if he could. I told Tony to come on out to the club and we would get them on the course.

A short time later they arrived at the club and went to the locker room to put on their shoes. I had arranged to get them on our Presidents Course. Tony invited me to play with them, but I was busy and told them I appreciated their invitation but I had some paper work to catch up on. I went to the first tee and got them started, then returned to my office.

After about an hour, Tony Lema and Tony Bennett came back into my office to thank me for getting them on the course but they had decided to quit. When I questioned them on their reason for quitting, Tony Lema told me that after a couple of holes, word had spread around the course that they were on the Presidents Course and that people began coming from all over the course to watch them play. Tony said they felt very bad about disrupting the members' games. They thought the best thing to do was to come in so the members could go back to the courses and continue their games.

I always felt bad about the members ruining their game. This was what I had tried to prevent when Tony came to the club. I wanted to make him feel he could come to the club and be treated like any other member. I think for the most part we had accomplished this until he came out on a busy weekend and brought a celebrity with him. This does show you the thoughtfulness of Tony Lema.

## Nicklaus at Greenbrier

We played the 1979 Ryder Cup Matches at the Greenbrier Resort in White Sulphur Springs, West Virginia. Jack Nicklaus had redesigned the golf course especially for the tournament. The Chesapeake Railroad System owned the Greenbrier Resort. We were having the dedication of the course in the spring of that year. The matches were scheduled to be played in the fall.

We had a big luncheon and invited some dignitaries from the West Virginia Golf Association, the USGA, and the PGA as well as other friends at the Greenbrier. At the luncheon, Jack reviewed all the changes that had been made to the golf course. After lunch, he gave a clinic after which we were going to play the golf course.

Don Padgett, the President of the PGA, asked me to play with Nicklaus, Joe DiMaggio, and Jim O'Keefe, who was an attorney from Chicago. Jim O'Keefe was on the PGA Advisory Committee as well as the Board of Directors of the Chesapeake Railroad Systems. Jack was the one who had convinced the Greenbrier to extend an invitation to host the Ryder Cup. The four of us were going to be the featured group.

After the clinic we had a ribbon cutting ceremony at the first tee. As is the custom, Jack hit the first drive and then I hit my drive. DiMaggio and O'Keefe hit their drives, playing from the forward markers. Jack and I played from the back tee. After our drives, we went down the fairway to our balls and Joe DiMaggio and Jack O'Keefe hit their second shots. I stood in the fairway waiting on Jack Nicklaus who stood over by a bunker with Jim Searle, the Director of Sports at the Greenbrier.

Jack was discussing a change he would like to make to the bunker. Jack looked over at me and said, "Go ahead and hit it, Joe. I'll be over there in a minute."

I said, "I would Jack, but it's not my turn."

When he walked by me, he said, "You kind of jumped on that one didn't you?"

As we continued to play I out-hit Jack on every hole. After we played about six holes, Jack said, "You know I checked on you before we played and was told you were a pretty good player, but I had no idea you could play this good. Why did you quit playing the tour?"

I said, "I couldn't putt, Jack."

He said, "Aw, we all say that!"

When we got to the 18$^{th}$ hole, I had three birdies and an eagle. I was beating Jack by a couple of strokes. The 18$^{th}$ hole was a par 5, dog leg right, and I had the honors. I hit a really good drive and when Jack got up to hit his drive, you could see that he was tired of me out driving him. He tried to hit the ball extra hard and hooked his shot over into the trees to the left and had to lay up short of the green.

I took my 3 wood and knocked it right in the middle of the green. We got on the green and I hit my eagle putt and as it got close to the hole, he hit my ball back to me and said, "We don't count scores in deals like this."

## Ryder Cup at Greenbrier

The 1979 Ryder Cup Matches were played at the Greenbrier Resort in White Sulphur Springs, West Virginia. There were a couple of significant changes made in the matches introduced that year. First, the British team was expanded to include all of the players who were playing on the European Tour. This brought about the need to change the name to the European Ryder Cup team. This change was made with the encouragement of the American PGA. There was a concern that the matches would become an insignificant event in the United States because the British team had not been competitive for several years. In fact, the last time the United States team had lost was in 1957. With this change, Seve Ballesteros and Antonio Garrido of Spain made the team.

The second change was not considered significant at the time. It was more of a procedural change. There had not been any provision in the agreement addressing what would happen if a player on either team became ill or were injured after the competition began. It was decided that if this occurred during the first two days, the injured or ill player could be replaced by one of the players on the team who was not selected to play in that particular match. However, for the singles match, a different procedure was needed because all players on both teams played in the singles matches.

The procedure that was adopted required the Captain of each team, prior to the announcement of the draw for the singles matches, to place the name of the player he wanted to sit out the matches in an envelope. If there was an injury or illness on either team, the player's name in the envelope of the team which was not affected by an injury or illness would sit out the singles match and he and the injured player would be deemed to have halved their match and each team would each receive ½ point. The player who was scheduled to play the injured or ill player would play the player who was scheduled to play the player whose name was in the envelope. If there was an injury or illness after the matches began, the ill or injured player would lose the match.

The idea behind the envelope was to protect either team from losing one of their top players if there was an injury or illness. The thought was that each Captain would place the name in the envelope of the player he thought was his weakest player. Billy Casper was Captain of the American team and John Jacobs was the European Captain. The new procedure was explained to each of the Captains prior to the start of the matches so they could consider who they would place in the envelope on Saturday before the draw was made for the singles matches.

As fate would have it, the envelope rule was needed the first year that it was implemented. Mark James, of the European Team, was injured after the draw was made for the singles matches and would not be able to play in the final round. This meant the player that Billy Casper had placed in the envelope would not play in the singles matches and would receive a half point as would Mark James.

The officials from the European Team advised the American Team officials that Mark James was injured. A meeting was held to open the envelope that Casper had provided to determine who would be dropped from the matches. When the envelope was opened the name revealed was Lee Trevino. Everyone was shocked. Trevino was clearly one of the top players on the American Team.

When the envelope procedure was explained to Casper, he indicated that he had misunderstood the purpose of the envelope and chose Trevino, thinking he was to place the name of the player he wanted to protect from being dropped from the match. When Casper explained to John Jacobs why Trevino's name was in the envelope, he asked John to let him change the name in the envelope. John did not respond immediately but asked for a few minutes to think about the request. He left the meeting and did not return for a couple of hours. When he finally returned, he allowed Casper to substitute Gil Morgan for Trevino. This was a wonderful show of sportsmanship on the part of Jacobs.

When asked later why he took so long to allow Casper to change his pick in the envelope, he said he talked to each member of his team to get their advice. It just took that long to contact all of the team members. It was a team decision.

Gil Morgan and Mark James were each awarded ½ point. Lee Trevino beat Sandy Lyle 2 and 1. The United States Ryder Cup Team won the matches 17 to 11. The envelope was used again in 1991 and 1993 due to injuries to European players.

## Tony and Betty Lema

Tony Lema met his wife Betty on an American Airlines flight. Betty was a flight attendant. After they were married they lived in Dallas. Tony had been living in Oakland, California, his home town, but because Dallas was the home base of American Airlines they decided to make Dallas their home. Even though they did not have children, there was a good part of the time that Betty did not travel with Tony due to her schedule at American Airlines.

Tony had been given the name" Champagne Tony" because when he won his first tournament on the tour, he had ordered champagne for all of the media in the press room. He had told the media at his press conference on Saturday night after the third round of the tournament, that if he won the next day, he would buy champagne for all.

One night in Dallas, after returning from a flight, Betty was on the way home on the Stemmons Freeway during a rain storm when she had a flat tire. She got out of the car to try to flag down someone to help her fix the flat. It was not long before a Good Samaritan stopped and changed the flat for her. When he finished, Betty got his business card from him and they both went on their way.

When Tony returned home from the tour, Betty told him about the man who had stopped and fixed her flat for her and said they should send him a gift. Tony agreed. A couple of days later the man's doorbell rang. When he went to answer the door, there was Betty and Tony Lema with several bottles of champagne. Tony told him that he appreciated what he had done to help Betty with her flat. He said, "I brought the champagne, let's have a party!"

After the man and his family got over the shock, a good time was had by all.

## Mickey Mantle

Mickey Mantle was a good friend. Because he also lived in Dallas, we got to see each other often. I met him through Billy Maxwell. Mickey had been a member at Preston Trail Golf Club from the time it first opened. On Mondays, we used to go to Jim Berrigan's Bar and they would cook up some beans and cornbread for us. Monday was normally a slow day for them. Then we would go out to Preston Trail and play golf. We became good friends.

When it was time for baseball season to start, we would be playing golf and riding in a cart. Then he would jump out and run 100 yards and jump back in the cart. I asked him what he was doing and he said, "Well, I'm training for baseball."

He was so strong he never hit a driver or wood. He played with a one iron. He could hit that one iron so far you couldn't believe it. He could play golf pretty well. He loved the game and I always thought he was a neat guy.

## Turned Down by Ben Hogan

Ben Hogan was a very nice man and he was always great to me. When I was Chairman of the Championship at Oakland Hills in 1979, I thought it would be great to get Ben to come for the Past Champions event because he had won the Open at Oakland Hills in 1951. He shot 67 in the last round and was the only one to break 70 during the tournament. When he won, his comment was, "I finally brought this monster to its knees." To this day, Oakland Hills is known as "The Monster."

I wrote him a letter inviting him to the Championship. He wrote back and said he just didn't want to go. But I decided I wasn't going to give up. I arranged a dinner with Shelley Mayfield, Ben, and I. Shelley was a good friend and someone who had played the tour with Ben and Golf Professional at Brookhollow Golf Club. I had even spoken to Valerie, Ben's wife, and she knew I was going to make my pitch. I wasn't going to give up on Ben.

As we were having dinner, I was all prepared to make my pitch. I said, "Ben there is one thing I want to talk to you about."

Valerie said, "Now Ben, you listen to Joe."

So I made my pitch and Ben looked at me with those steely blue eyes and said, "Joe, I don't care if I ever leave Fort Worth again."

That took care of that!

## Tony Lema at Brookhaven

When Tony Lema moved to Dallas, I gave him an honorary membership in Brookhaven Country Club in Dallas where I was the Director of Golf. Tony and I had been good friends when I was playing the tour as well as while I was running the tour. It can be awkward when a touring pro first moves to a new city to find a place to play and practice. He has to be in the community long enough to establish relationships where he can ask to use certain facilities for the purpose of working on his game while in town. He also needs someone to shield him from too much attention from the members. I had done the same thing for Billy Maxwell. Tony had been an assistant professional at a club prior to going on the tour, and was well versed in how to be a member of a club.

When Tony was in town, he would usually call me and suggest we play a round of golf. He was what you would consider a perfect member. When he arrived at the club, he would come to the golf shop and buy a dozen balls prior to the round. This was something he did not have to do because he was provided free balls from Titleist, who paid him to use their balls. He did this because he thought all members should support their golf professional and he wanted to set an example for the members. Obviously this was not lost on the members.

When we would play, we would usually have quite a few of

the members follow us. This always made Tony feel bad because he knew the members had come to the club to play or to work on their own game. I had to keep assuring him that it was a real thrill for the members to be able to see him play, and it helped me with the members to see him

"If there was ever a perfect club member, it was Tony Lema."

coming to the club to play with me.

At the conclusion of the round, Tony would always pay for my caddy as well as his as we walked to the clubhouse from the 18th green. He wanted all of the members following us to see this. He was trying to set an example for the members. He felt if the professional played with the members, they should pay their caddy fee.

When we would go to the club room and grill to settle our bets, he would insist on buying the first round of drinks. He would also stay for a few minutes to talk to the other members we played with as well as other in the grill who would ask him questions about the tour and about other tour players.

If ever there was a perfect club member, it was Tony Lema.

## Significant Events in Golf 1970-1979

**Deane Beman:** Maybe one of the most significant events in the history of the modern PGA Tour was the appointment of Deane Beman as Commissioner in 1974. During his tenure as the Commissioner, he shepherded a tremendous number of innovative changes to the tour while increasing the purses to unbelievable heights. Some of the most important changes included the all exempt tour, development of the Champions Tour and the Nationwide Tour, and creation of the TPC Golf Course network. He also created the agronomic division of the tour which provided the expertise for sponsors to improve the conditioning of the tour golf courses. One of the many reasons for the improved scoring on the tour was the improved conditioning of the golf courses.

He also introduced the concept of stadium golf and built the first stadium course at Ponte Vedra, Florida. He brought awareness to the role of PGA Tour in raising huge sums of money for charity in all of the communities where tour tournaments are played. Beman also developed corporate involvement in golf to a new level through the creative use of partnerships between corporate involvement and television.

**Television:** There were several improvements in television production that greatly enhanced the quality of televised golf. The most significant of these were the slow motion camera, hand held cameras, instant replay, and aerial television cameras. The television networks also found that even though the ratings of television golf were not as high as other sports such as football and baseball, they attracted corporate support for the telecast from a wide range of corporations who found that the profile of the television viewer was the target market they were trying to reach with their message. These companies included banking, financial services, insurance companies and other companies that provide goods and services to more upscale consumers.

**Improvement in Equipment:** There were many significant improvements in golf equipment in the 1970's that directly affected the playing of the game. Most notable were metal woods, perimeter weighting of clubs, big-headed drivers, and cast method of making club heads. There were improvements in the manufacturing of golf balls as well as golf shafts. This included the introduction of new material in golf club manufacturing. Some of the material included graphite, titanium, stainless steel, aluminum, and a blend of these materials. The improvements in the golf ball included dimple patterns, the development of the multi-layered ball, and the durable covers.

**Lightning Detectors:** When you tune into a televised golf tournament today and there is inclement weather, the tournament is usually stopped and players either taken off the course or take shelter in designated areas on the course prior to the bad weather arriving. The reason this is possible is that the tour has a weather trailer and two meteorologists that travel with the tour. The trailer is equipped with virtually all the same equipment that would normally be found in the weather department at your local TV station.

When I was running the tour in 1963 we had a thunderstorm at the Buick Open in Grand Blanc, Michigan. One of the spectators was struck by lighting and killed. Even though we had stopped play prior to the incident we often wished we had a better way to track inclement weather.

In 1976, we played the PGA Championship at Congressional Country Club in Washington, D.C. A Swedish Company contacted us about using a new machine they had developed that could track lighting storms and give us an alert prior to the storm arriving in the area. Even though we were skeptical that the machine would work, we accepted their offer. As luck would have it, we had a thunderstorm on Friday afternoon. The operator of the machine called me on the radio to tell me the storm was approaching. I blew the horn and suspended play getting the players off the course and telling the gallery to take cover.

Everyone thought I was crazy as it was a clear beautiful day. However a few minutes later a huge thunderstorm moved through the area. Now I was a genius. Today not only are there lighting detectors at each golf tournament, but most of the golf courses in the country also have lighting detectors.

**Senior Tour:** Fred Rafael and Jimmy Demaret held a golf tournament at Onion Creek Country Club, in Austin, Texas. They invited all of the former senior tour players to play a televised four ball tournament. The tournament and the telecast were a huge success. The gallery and the television audience really enjoyed seeing their hero's from the past competing again. By 1980, the Senior Tour was born and is now known as the Champions Tour. When the Senior Tour was born, the average player on the tour only played until they reached an age of the mid thirty's to early forties. The Senior Tour has made it possible for a lifetime career for the current tournament player.

**Uniform Rules of Golf:** The United States Golf Association and the Royal and Ancient Golf Club of St. Andrews the two principle rules bodies of the world reached agreement in the 1970's to a uniform Rules of Golf. Prior to that, each body had most of the same rules but had disagreements on some of the rules due to different playing conditions and just a different philosophy of how the game should be played. I had the good fortunate to serve as a consulting member of the USGA Rules Committee representing the PGA of America during this time. It was really the right thing to do. Now people can play around the world and not have to worry about learning a different set of rules.

**Stimpmeter:** Though developed in the mid 1930's, the Stimpmeter did not come into prominence until it was first used at the U.S. Open at the Atlanta Athletic Club. The Stimpmeter is a simple metal strip that you roll a ball down to measure the speed of the green. The ball is rolled down the device with the grain of the green and in the opposite direction. The length the ball rolls in each direction is measured and averaged and that number becomes the speed of the green.

**Teaching the Game:** One of the primary responsibilities of the members of PGA of America is the teaching and growing of the game. The two responsibilities go hand in hand. By teaching the game, pupils learn to play better and as a result play more golf and enjoy it more. The satisfied pupil also encourages friend and family to take up the game. Over the years the PGA has conducted many teaching seminars to train the professional to become better teachers. These seminars are usually taught by professionals who have gained a reputation as exceptional teachers.

Over time, professionals interested in teaching the game have developed all types of aids to help teaching the game. Many of them were developed in the 1970's. Some of these devices have become very prominent. One of the first such devices was the sequence camera which would take six still pictures during one swing. This was great for showing the pupil what was taking place through the sequence of his swing. Another important device was the video camera which gave the professional the ability to film the pupils swing and immediately review the swing with the pupil. The pupil could take the video with him to review at his leisure and to review progress from lesson to lesson. When the stop action camera came along it enhanced the use of the video camera.

A part of teaching of the game is fitting of the club to the player. The task is to fit the loft and lie of the club to the player as well as the length and grip size. With this came the development of a bending machine that could adjust the loft and lie of the club. This machine had an electrical motor and would bend the club to the desired adjustment. More modern equipment now monitors the launch angle and speed of the ball. The development of these devices has provided great tools to help the golf professional teach the game.

**The Ryder Cup:** The 1977 Ryder Cup Matches were played at Royal Lytham and St. Annes Golf Club in St. Annes, England. By 1977 the Ryder Cup Matches had diminished in popularity in the United States to the degree that the TV Networks in the United States did not want to broadcast the matches. In fact the only way we could get ABC to show the matches was to package the Ryder Cup Matches and the PGA Championship. If they wanted to televise the Championship they had to televise the Ryder Cup Matches. They even offered to pay us not to require them to televise the matches.

When we arrived at Royal Lytham and St. Annes, Henry Poe, the Past President of the PGA, and Don Padgett, the President, had a meeting with The Earl of Derby, the President of the British PGA. Henry and Don told Lord Derby the only way the matches could survive was to expand the British team to include all players on the European Tour. Jack Nicklaus spoke to Lord Derby and told him the same thing. Lord Derby told the American PGA that he would bring the issue up with the British PGA Board of Directors. After a meeting of the British PGA Board they agreed to expand the team to include players on the European Tour.

At the 1979 matches played at The Greenbrier Resort in White Sulphur Springs, West Virginia, there were two players from the European Tour, Seve Ballesteros and Anthony Garrido who made the team. Ballesteros embraced the matches with such a passion that it energized the whole team. By 1983 the matches had become so competitive that the United States won by one point. In 1985 the European team won for the first time in 28 years and in 1987 won on American soil for the first time ever.

Today the Ryder Cup Matches are the biggest event in golf and one of the biggest events in the world of sports.

# Decade of the 80's

## A Hole in One at Las Colinas

In the late 1970's, The Gatlin Brothers and the Dallas Metropolitan Assistant Golf Professionals teamed up to put on the Gatlin Brothers Muscular Dystrophy Pro-Am to raise money to fight Muscular Dystrophy. The event was led by Rudy Gatlin, representing the Gatlin Brothers, and Randy Smith, the Assistant Professional at Royal Oaks Country Club. Randy is now the long time head professional at Royal Oaks and one of the top golf Instructors in the world.

The marketing effort was a collaboration of both organizations, with the assistant professionals having the responsibility of conducting the play of the tournament. The Gatlin Brothers used their contacts in the music industry to bring together an incredible list of celebrities to play in the tournament as well as to participate in the entertainment and a gala dinner Monday night after the tournament. The tournament was a huge success and a large amount of money was raised for Muscular Dystrophy research for several years.

In 1982, my final year as President of the PGA of America, I was fortunate enough to have my good friend Darrell Royal as the celebrity in my group. Darrell was the former football coach at the University of Texas and larger than life to most Texans. Playing in front of us was Ben Crenshaw with Larry Gatlin and behind us was U.S. Open Champion David Graham with movie star Jim Garner. Most of the amateurs playing in all three groups were friends and had friendly bets with each other as to the final outcome between the groups.

We were playing the tournament at the Las Colinas Country Club in Irving, Texas. Las Colinas is a wonderful club with a great golf course. When we reached the par three 13th hole, there was a delay on the tee due to the slow play created by the oversubscription of participants in the tournament. The 13th hole at Las Colinas is a short hole with an elevated tee playing to a green set next to a lake. The length of the hole was 155 yards but played shorter due to the elevation change from the tee to the green. When our group arrived at the 13th tee, Ben Crenshaw and his group was waiting to tee off. After they completed the hole, they waited on the back of the green to watch our shots to the green.

Our first player hit his shot on the green but not near the hole. Our second player hit his shot on the green inside our first player's ball. Our third player also hit the green again nearer the hole than the previous two players. It was now Darrell Royal's turn and his shot ended up only four feet from the hole.

By this time David Graham and his group had finished the 12th hole and were standing behind the tee watching our group hit their tee shots. There was a lot of conversation from David and his group telling me the pressure was on since each of my team had hit the ball nearer the hole on a progressive basis. I selected a 9 iron for my shot and hit a very good shot. In fact it looked so good I yelled, "Get in the hole!"

The ball landed on the green behind the hole but drew back into the hole. Crenshaw and Gatlin started yelling as did everyone on the tee. I have never seen any group have each shot be progressively nearer the hole with the last one being a hole in one.

Because of that hole in one, our team won the Gatlin Brothers Pro-Am.

# Vice President Bush and the Grand Slam of Golf

The Grand Slam of Golf was started in 1979. It was suggested by then PGA President Don Padgett, as a fund raiser for the PGA Junior Golf Foundation. The Junior Golf Foundation was also the creation of Don, who had a real passion for Junior Golf and made it one of the centerpieces of his presidency. Don felt the PGA should enhance its position as the national leader of introducing juniors to the game by creating a tax deductible entity to receive contributions for promoting junior golf. A part of this initiative was to start the Boys and Girls PGA Junior Championships. He felt that the PGA should pay the expenses of the participants so that regardless of the economic situation of a junior golfers' family, they would be able to participate in the Championship.

The plan we developed was really quite simple. We would ask the winners of the four Major Championships to donate a day to the PGA to raise money for junior golf. Thus, the Grand Slam of Golf was born. In 1981, the third playing of the Grand Slam was scheduled at Breakers

Vice President George Bush and Lee Trevino

West Country Club in Palm Beach, Florida. The winners of the four Major Championships in 1980 were Jack Nicklaus (the U.S. Open Champion), Seve Ballesteros (the Masters Champion), Tom Watson (the British Open Champion) and Lee Trevino (the PGA Champion). With a premier group like this, there was a lot of interest by the golfing public to attend the match. We had decided to limit the gallery to four thousand who would be required to make a $25 donation to the Junior Golf Foundation in order to attend. The matches were a sellout.

A short time before the matches were to be played, we received an inquiry from Vice President George Bush's office to see if it would be alright for the Vice President and Mrs. Bush to attend the matches. Vice President Bush was going to be in Palm Beach attending a fund raising luncheon. Of course, we immediately agreed. We were told that they would be arriving late due to the timing of the luncheon he was attending. We were delighted to invite the Bush's to the matches because we felt it would enhance the reputation of the matches. Besides, who could refuse the Vice President of the United States of America?

The day of the matches was quite windy. After we started, Mark Kizziar and Mickey Powell, the two other officers of the PGA, Frank Cardi, our Honorary President, and Mark Cox, our Executive Director, and I remained at the clubhouse to welcome Vice President and Mrs. Bush. By the time the Bushes arrived, the players had completed the first nine holes and were playing on the back nine. When the Bush limousine arrived, Mrs. Bush jumped out of the car and asked, "Where are they Joe?"

This surprised me because I had never met Mrs. Bush. I had asked Frank Cardi to escort Mrs. Bush, so I introduced her to Frank and told her Frank would be her escort. She replied, "Come on Frank, let's go".

We had been told that the Vice President would still be in his suit and would like to change into a golf shirt before he went onto the course. We had arranged for a locker for him and had placed three shirts in the locker. Of course, the shirts had the PGA logo on them. When he got out of the car and introductions were made, he said, "I brought my photographer with me, why don't we get the picture taking out of the way first?"

I told him we had our photographer also, so we could get right to the picture taking. After we completed the picture taking session and he changed clothes, we got on a golf cart and headed out to the course. When we arrived at the hole where the players were, I told him we would drive under the ropes and drive along with the players. He replied, "Why don't we walk?"

So we abandoned the cart and joined the players. After introductions were made, the Vice President was invited to hit a couple of shots. He struck the ball pretty well for having not played for awhile.

While we were walking the last few holes with the players, he had a great conversation with all of the players. As we walked along, I asked him if he would join me in presenting the trophy to the winner. He readily agreed as long as Mrs. Bush could join us on the dais. After the round was completed and our staff had scrambled to rearrange the seating on the dais, I introduced the Vice President and gave a brief history of his family's involvement with golf. I told about his grandfather, George Herbert Walker, a former President of the United States Golf Association who donated the trophy for the Walker Cup Matches. I also mentioned that his uncle, Prescott Bush, had also been President of the USGA. He was quite surprised that I knew of his family involvement in the game. I also told the gallery that it had been a pretty good day for Texas. The Vice President was from Texas, I was also from Texas, as was Lee Trevino who shot 68 to win the Grand Slam.

After the presentation was over, Tom Watson came to me and asked me if I would ask Vice President Bush if he could ride back to the Breakers Hotel where the Bushes as well as the players were staying. We had a fund raising dinner that night at the Breakers. Tom did not like to fly in a helicopter, which was the arrangement we had made for the players so they would have plenty of time to prepare for dinner. President Bush was very pleased to accommodate Tom. I often wondered what the conversation was on the way to the hotel. Tom was probably the most liberal player on the tour and of course Vice President Bush was ultra conservative.

## Dick Bator Oak Hills Country Club

As the National Secretary of the PGA of America, one of my responsibilities was to be the General Chairman of the PGA Championship. This entailed several trips to Rochester, N.Y., to visit the Oak Hills Country Club, site of the 1980 PGA Championship. The condition of the golf course is always one of the great concerns. A stipulation in the contract for all of our championships is that we have complete control of the golf course and are able to set the maintenance procedures for conditioning the course. This includes determining the height of cut for the greens, tees, fairways, and roughs, as well as the depth of sand in the bunkers, and when the sand is to be installed.

Dick Bator was the golf course superintendent at Oak Hills. He truly is one of the best superintendents in the country. However, Dick and I did not agree with the height of cut for the greens and fairways. He was afraid that if it got hot and humid during the tournament that it would create a problem to maintain the health of the grass. I told him that I would like the greens cut at 1/8 inch and the fairways at 1/2 inch. I also told him I would like the sand in the bunkers to be a maximum of three inches deep and for the sand on the slopes of the bunkers to be hand packed so that a ball would not plug in the face of the bunkers. We wanted all of the sand installed in the fall, prior to the tournament, so that it would have time to settle and become firm for the tournament.

Dick decided that three inches of sand was not sufficient, so he installed six inches in the fall prior to the tournament. He thought that when the sand became compacted it would shrink down to three inches by the following spring. When I came to Oak Hills for my spring visit there was far too much sand in the bunkers. I told Dick he was going to have to remove enough sand to bring the bunkers down to a depth of three inches.

This became a huge project for Dick and he had to hire a special crew to do nothing except remove the sand. I suggested to Dick that he could stockpile the sand and not have to buy any for several years. As the summer began, the sand project became a source of a great deal of kidding between Dick and me. He also had a lot of reservations about the height of the cut for the greens, so there was bantering back and forth between us. By the time of the championship, the golf course was in superb condition.

When I advised the Oak Hill transportation committee of my travel schedule so they could meet my plane, Dick asked if he could be the one to meet me at the airport. When I deplaned at the Rochester Airport, I was surprised to see Dick there to greet me. He had a paper bag in his hand and told me he wanted to present me with a couple of welcoming gifts. He then removed from the bag a large plastic cylinder filled with sand and a small square of cut sod from one of the putting greens. He gave them to me with the instructions to use the sand as a suppository and the turf as a wig.

I roared with laughter. It was a great joke.

## Dave Marr – Ryder Cup Captain

The Officers of the PGA have the honor of recommending to the Board of Directors the proposed Captain of the Ryder Cup Team. As the President of the PGA in 1981, I brought up the subject to Mark Kizziar and Mickey Powell, my fellow Officers. The two names I suggested were Julius Boros and Gene Littler. Both players had been members of numerous Ryder Cup Teams, and both had won Major Championships. Littler had won the U.S. Open, and Boros had won the U.S. Open twice, as well as the PGA Championship. Both were criteria that we had established in order to be considered for the position. After a fair amount of discussion, we decided that we would invite Julius Boros to be the Captain of the 1981 Ryder Cup Team.

The President had the task of calling the person selected to become the Captain to inform him of his selection. It is considered quite an honor to serve as Captain of the team. In fact many of the past Captains feel it is the highlight of their career. All of the great players in the past had been Captain. Many of them such as Walter Hagen, Ben Hogan, Arnold Palmer, Sam Snead, and Jack Nicklaus served at least twice. It was not unusual for players who felt they deserved to be the Captain to lobby for the position. In fact, this still goes on today.

I made the call to Julius Boros to tell him of our selection of him as the Captain of the team. After I told him of our choice and congratulated him on his selection, there was a moment of silence on the phone. He then told me that he was going to decline the invitation. He said he did not like to give speeches and he knew the Captain had to give a lot of speeches in representing the team. He said he would not be comfortable doing that. He added that he appreciated the thought and knew it was a great honor but he thought we should select someone else.

I then talked to Mark Kizziar and Mickey Powell again, and we agreed to Invite Gene Littler to be the Captain. I called Gene and extended the invitation to him. Gene also declined. He had the same reservations as Julius Boros: he did not like to do public speaking and felt he would not do a good job. He thanked me and wished the team the best of luck. I have never heard of a player declining to be the Captain of the Ryder Cup Team before 1981 and I have not heard of one since.

We went back to the drawing board for the third time to determine who should be the Captain. There were several names brought up without a consensus. After a few minutes I suggested Dave Marr. Dave had not won many tournaments on the tour but he had won the PGA Championship and had played on one Ryder Cup Team. I knew he loved the Ryder Cup Matches. He and I had talked about the matches and what a great thrill it was to play on the team with Byron Nelson as the Captain. I also knew that Dave was very popular with the players and that his selection would be well received. We agreed to select Dave Marr.

I called Dave to tell him of his being our choice to Captain the team. Again there was silence when I informed him of our choice. But, then he began to cry. He told me he had always dreamed of being the Captain of the team but he had never thought he would have the opportunity. He promised me he would be one of the best Captains we had ever had. Dave was not only a great Captain, but the 1981 Ryder Cup Team may have been one of the best, if not the best team we have ever fielded. Every player on the team except Bruce Lietzke had won a major championship.

## TPA PGA Tour

After several months of discussions, the PGA Tour Tournament Policy Board, meeting at the 1981 World Series of Golf, voted to change the name of the tour to the Tournament Players Association Tour. The reason for this change was the desire of Deane Beman, the Commissioner of the Tour, to expand the Tour marketing opportunities to include soft goods. Deane felt the tour could develop a substantial income stream from the sale of merchandise with the PGA Tour logo. Beman had no interest in going into the hard goods marketing because of the endorsement relationships the individual players had with the golf manufacturers.

The Tournament Policy Board was comprised of four tour players, the three officers of the PGA of America, and three independent businessmen. As Officers of the PGA, we had to oppose the program for legal reasons. The PGA had a long-term agreement with the PGA Golf Equipment Company for use of all of the PGA and Ryder Cup trademarks for both golf hard goods and soft goods. This precluded the tour from embarking on a soft good program using the PGA trade mark. We were also opposed to changing the name of the tour. However Deane Beman prevailed in the debate and the named was changed to the Tournament Players Association Tour and the initials TPA used for brevity.

In January of 1982, I received a call from Deane telling me he was going to be in Dallas and wanted to know if I would like to have dinner. I invited him to eat with me at Brookhaven. During dinner, Deane broached the subject of trying to find a way to return the name of the tour to the PGA tour. I told Deane that I would be willing to explore the possibility, but that I would not negotiate in the media. All of our meetings would have to be secret. We would have to meet in out of the way places and at odd times to try to maintain the secrecy of the meetings. I told him if the secrecy was breeched we would discontinue the meetings.

I have often thought about what problems made Deane feel the need to put the name back on the tour. I think he found that TPA was not playing well with the tournament sponsors, who would have to spend a lot of money to change their signage and marketing tools. I also think when he approached the soft goods manufacturers, he did not get a warm reception. I think their concerns were that their TPA Tour products would not be well received in the golf shops by the PGA professionals. In some instances, I think there was some resistance from the players who felt their opportunities for endorsement deals with the soft goods manufacturers would be affected.

Our first meeting of the Tour Policy Board to begin the negotiations was held in a small branch bank in Palm Beach Gardens, Florida, at seven on a Sunday morning. There were other issues that we wanted to address as well as the marketing issues. The all exempt tour was due to be implemented in 1983, which meant that club professionals would lose a number of opportunities to qualify to play on the tour. There was also the possible loss of revenue to the PGA if we were able to renegotiate our agreement with PGA Golf Company to permit the tour to use our trade mark for soft goods. Because of the legal issues involved, it was decided to include the legal counsel on both sides in the meetings. The PGA Attorneys were Bill Rogers and Steve Sacks, from Arnold and Porter of Washington, D.C, and the tour counsel was Bill Rogers, of Rogers and Wells, also of Washington.

After the first meeting in Palm Beach Gardens, meetings were held in Jacksonville, Florida, New York, Washington, D.C., Los Angeles, and finally back at Jacksonville. Through these various meetings, an agreement was ultimately hammered out. The major points were to change the name of the tour back to the PGA Tour. There would be a new ten tournament tour, each with a purse of $100,000 to be funded jointly by the PGA Tour and the PGA of America. These tournaments would provide spots for fifty club Professionals and fifty non-exempt tour players. There would be a new marketing entity created, PGA/PGA Tour Properties, owned jointly by The PGA of America and the PGA Tour, with profits shared equally.

The hard part for me was to convince Bob MacNally, the President of PGA Golf Company, to renegotiate our agreement to permit PGA/PGA Tour Golf Properties to use the PGA Trademark in order to market PGA Tour soft goods. We had one thing going for us. PGA Golf had a soft goods line, but it was being marketed under the Mark Scott label rather than under the PGA label. We were also fortunate in being able to negotiate with Bob MacNally. Bob was a good friend who understood the big picture and felt it would be better for the tour to carry the PGA name. Of course there were a lot of legal issues so we had to have both of our attorneys involved in order to draft the proposed changes to the contract.

We concluded our negotiations with the Tour Policy Board at our regular meeting at tour headquarters in Jacksonville on the Tuesday before the TPC Championship. We then began negotiating with Bob MacNally. He would not come to Jacksonville from his headquarters in Chicago so we had to negotiate on the phone and fax documents back and forth. We commandeered Deane Beman's office at tour headquarters to handle the negations with MacNally. The negotiations dragged on well into the evening, but we finally completed them and approved the final draft. I signed the agreement and faxed it to Bob and he signed it and faxed a copy back to me. After three months of secret negotiations the deal was finally done.

On March 19th, the morning of the second round of the TPC, there were special announcements posted on the scoreboards around the course announcing the return of the name of the tour back to the PGA Tour. Deane Beman, Bob Oelman the Chairman of the Policy Board, Mark Kizziar the Secretary of the PGA, PGA Treasurer Mickey Powell, and I held a press conference to announce the agreement. The press conference lasted forty-five minutes where all of the details were outlined to the media. We never had to answer one question from the media prior to that press conference. Quite an accomplishment!

## Lee Trevino & Jerry Pate at the Ryder Cup Matches

The 1981 Ryder Cup Matches were played at Walton Heath Golf Club just outside of London. During one of his press interviews, Lee Trevino told the media that Jerry Pate was probably one of the best players in the world from the neck down. He said if he could do all of the thinking for Jerry he would be an unbelievable player. Surprisingly Jerry did not take offense with the remark. He thought it was funny. Captain Dave Marr saw the remarks made by Trevino and decided to pair them together the next day in the four ball matches.

When they arrived at the first tee the next day and it came Jerry's turn to play, he took a driver from his bag. The first hole was a short par four. A driver would put Jerry too close to the green for an effective second shot. The second shot would have been less than a full shot and it would be hard to stop the ball on the small hard greens. Trevino reached over and took the driver out of Jerry's hand and gave him a 3-wood. He told him to hit a nice control cut which would leave him with a full sand wedge second shot. Jerry hit a good tee shot and proceeded to hit the second shot close and made a birdie.

From that point forward for the rest of the match, Trevino would give Jerry the club he wanted him to hit and tell him the type shot he wanted him to play. After the 12th hole, the match was over with the American side winning 7 and 5 over Nick Faldo and Sam Torrance. Jerry Pate had made eight birdies. Trevino did not allow Jerry forget that the rest of the trip.

## Ryder Cup Speech

The United States team arrived in Britain on a September Monday morning in 1981. The Matches were played at Walton Heath Golf Club, Surrey, England. After motoring to the Club from London, Dave Marr, the captain of the American Team, gave the team the day off to get acclimated after the flight from New York. The matches were played on Friday through Sunday, with practice rounds played on Tuesday, Wednesday, and Thursday. Since there are only twelve players on each team, one team would practice in the morning and the other team would practice in the afternoon. This way there would be players on the course most of the day for the gallery to follow.

Dave Marr elected to practice in the morning and let his team have the opportunity to go to London in the afternoon for shopping and sightseeing. This decision received a lot of attention in the British media. They viewed this as arrogance on the part of the American team. They were pictured as being more on holiday than coming to play the Ryder Cup Matches. It was also inferred that the American team was over confident. There was also a lot of attention given to the amount of money the players and their wives were spending shopping. At that time, the world economy was not doing well and they seemed to feel the amount of money being spent by the American team was extravagant.

On Thursday afternoon, the opening ceremony is held with the teams introduced to the gallery, speeches by the Presidents of the British and American PGA, and the flags raised to the playing of the national anthems. The pairings for the Friday morning matches are then read by the President of the British PGA. After the pairings are read, the two teams and the officials of both parties are led off the stage by a bagpiper and the ceremonies are concluded.

During the ceremony, Lord Derby, the Earl of Derby, who was the President of the British PGA, made his remarks to the gallery. During his speech he commented on the media reports about the American team spending a lot of time in London shopping and sightseeing and seeming to be over confident. He felt that this would be the year that the European Team would win back the Ryder Cup. After Lord Derby finished his speech, I was introduced to make my remarks. After the usual remarks about how well we were being treated, comments about the course, etc., I concluded my speech by saying, "My Lord, I want to tell you one thing, we did not come to Great Britain to bail out the British economy and lose the Ryder Cup."

# The Texas Joe Black Cup Matches

In 1981, I received a call from Charlie Epps, the golf professional at Houston Country Club, asking me if I would lend my name to a planned match between the Northern and Southern Texas PGA Sections. The match format would be similar to the Ryder Cup Matches. The teams would be comprised of one touring professional, along with the President and the senior champion from each section. The balance of each team would be made up of the leading nine players selected from a point system used to judge performance in the major tournaments in each section. Over the years, making the Joe Black Cup Team has become the number one priority of most of the professionals in each section.

Texas Joe Black
Cup Trophy

The first matches were played at Westwood Golf Club in Houston. Dave Marr played for the Southern Texas Section team, and Rives McBee played for the Northern Texas Section team. This was the only year the touring professionals played in the matches. Over the years, we honored several people at the dinner on Sunday night prior to the first round of the matches. Some of those honored were Byron Nelson and Ben Hogan. At other times we have had people like Lanny Watkins and Jackie Burke speak at the dinner.

I did something special for the 25th anniversary of the Joe Black Cup matches. We had the matches at Barton Creek Country Club in Austin. When the matches started, I had no idea they would last for 25 years. We invited all of the past captains of both teams to come to the dinner on Sunday evening. We had a special money clip made which we presented to the past captains and the players who made the 25th Anniversary teams. We had 37 of the past captains attend. Unfortunately some of the former captains were deceased.

Usually the past captains were selected for their service to the PGA, whether it was on a national or a local basis. Some of the more prominent past captains who attended the dinner were Ross Collins, Jay McClure, and Jackson Bradley. All of these gentlemen had been very prominent in the national PGA during their careers.

We dispersed the two teams throughout the room seating then with the former captains. Many of these players had never met the former captains and had a great evening getting to know each other. The following day, all of the team members were talking about the past captains and relating the stories told at their tables.

When I retired from running the tour in 1964, a dinner was held at the last tournament of the year, the Haig and Haig Mixed Foursome, an event pairing members of the LPGA and PGA tour players in a mixed team event. At that dinner I was presented with a washed gold antique scotch dispenser. It was a replica of a dispenser made in 1740. The dispenser was mounted on a marble base and was in working order. The unique thing about the dispenser was that all of the actual signatures of the prominent players of 1964 had been engraved on the dispenser. This was really a special gift.

I decided that since the matches had lasted twenty-five years and had become such an important event in Texas I would retire the old permanent wooden trophy that had been presented to the winning team each year and donate the scotch dispenser as the new Joe Black Cup Matches trophy. It was unveiled at the dinner and made quite a hit.

## Palmer and Boros at the PGA National

The 1982 PGA Senior championship was moved from Turnberry Isle Country Club in North Miami, Florida, to the PGA National Golf Club at Palm Beach Gardens, Florida. At that time, the Senior Tour was fairly new and there was a lot of conversation about the length the courses should be played. I had talked to the Senior Tour Staff and got their input. I talked to several of the players as well.

After all of my research I decided to play the course at about 6700 yards. We advised the players that it was the yardage they could expect for all four days of the tournament. At that time, the belief was that the players could not shoot low enough scores to make the tournaments exciting for the gallery and that it would create a lot of bad publicity if the courses were set up to play at full length.

When the players started arriving at the PGA National, a lot of players had comments to make to me and the other PGA Officers about the yardage we planned to play. One school of thought was that this was a Major Championship and the course should be played at full length. The other side of the argument was that if the course was played at full length it would give too much of an advantage to a very few players. After listening to all of the arguments I decided to go ahead and play the course at the 6700 yards as announced.

There were two players in particular who gave me grief about the planned yardage. Every time I saw Arnold Palmer he would continue to argue for lengthening the course, even after the tournament started. Julius Boros was just the opposite. He thought the course should be played shorter. Even at 6700 yards he thought it gave too much of an advantage to just a few players, and that so many high scores would be shot that it would embarrass too many players.

It was my habit to stand on the first tee during the last round and thank the players for playing in the Championship and get any comments to be considered for the following years' tournaments. When the last group of players arrived at the tee I called them over and told Arnold and Julius, that in spite of all of their lobbying, we must have set the course up about right since they were tied with each other for the lead

.

# Jim O'Keefe Man of Year Award

In 1982, I received a call from Tom King, a member of the PGA Advisory Committee, asking me to attend a dinner in Chicago to honor another of our Advisory Committee members Jim O'Keefe, who had been selected Man of the Year for the city. The dinner fit well into my schedule because I had to be in Washington D.C. the next day to attend an Allied Associations of Golf meeting. The dinner was being held at the Palmer House in Chicago and Tom King told me a reservation would be made for me there and the details of the dinner would be at the front desk when I checked into the hotel.

When I registered for my room, I was given an envelope from Tom King. After I settled in and unpacked, I opened the letter. My instructions were to come to a small holding room off the ballroom where the dinner was being held. I was to remain there with some of the other dignitaries until he came to lead us to the head table where we would be seated for the dinner. This is when the evening took a strange turn.

When I arrived at the holding room, the only people in the room were former President Gerald Ford and a waiter. President Ford was a member of the PGA Advisory Committee but I had never met him. After introductions, we ordered a cocktail from the waiter and chatted until someone came to lead us to the dais to take our seats. As we arrived at the dais, we were introduced by Tom King, Master of Ceremony for the evening. Everyone else at the head table was already seated when we arrived.

President Ford was seated to the left of the podium next to Tom King and I was seated to the right next to the Governor of Illinois. I had not been told if I was going to have to make any remarks but had prepared some notes in the event I was asked to do so. Seated at the head table were many of the leading democrats from Chicago and the State of Illinois, including U.S. Congressman Dan Rostenkowski, who was also on the PGA Advisory Committee.

After Tom King introduced some of the dignitaries and made some remarks, dinner was served. After dessert and coffee, Tom again moved to the podium and started the program. It became apparent very quickly that the dinner was a huge fundraiser for the Democratic Party. Honoring Jimmy O'Keefe was the excuse for the fundraiser. Jim O'Keefe was a prominent attorney in Chicago and Mayor Daly's right hand man. The Merchandise Mart was owned by the Kennedy family and managed for them by Tom King. Neither President Ford nor I were asked to make any remarks and were only thanked by Tom at the conclusion of the dinner for our attendance.

After the dinner it was very apparent why President Ford and I were the only ones in the holding room and were not asked to speak. I can't understand why we were invited at all.

## Jack Nicklaus – Ryder Cup Captain

Jack Nicklaus was selected as captain of the 1983 Ryder Cup Team. At the time, he commented that the Captain's responsibilities were not too complicated. Other than giving a few speeches and making the pairings for the matches each round, his job would be to keep the players provided with Band-aids and ice water. Little did he know what would transpire before the end of the event.

The European Team arrived in Miami on a chartered Boeing 747 British Airways flight. The European Ryder Cup Committee had decided on the charter flight so they could sell the excess seats to their supporters at a price that would cover the airfare for their team and the official party that accompanied the team. The agreement between the European Ryder Cup Committee and the PGA of America provides that once the visiting team arrives on American soil their expenses are paid by the American PGA.

The package that the European Ryder Cup Committee had put together for their supporters included the flight on the charter with the team as well as hotel accommodations and badges to the matches. The only problem with their plan was that we were only required to provide them with badges for the 40 people in their official party. They requested another 100 to give to their supporters at no charge. They did not make this request until they arrived in the United States. We told them we could make the badges available to them but they would have to pay for them. Our contract with the local sponsor provided we receive a certain number of badges and all other badges we had to pay for.

This became a serious problem for the Europeans and created a lot of tension between our two organizations. After a good deal of discussion and a lot of badgering from the Europeans, we finally agreed to accommodate their request. It was a very gracious gesture provided by our local sponsors. Of course, this caused some resentment within the PGA.

Things went well for the next couple of days until the European Ryder Cup Committee dropped their next bomb. Jack Nicklaus had not been involved in the badge fiasco but was well aware of what had transpired. The next incident brought Nicklaus directly into discussions.

The Executive Director of the British PGA, Colin Snape, advised us on Thursday, the day before the matches were to begin, that if the matches were not completed on Sunday that they would not be able to stay over on Monday to finish. He said that their charter arrangement with British Airways provided for a return to London on Monday morning. With the matches being played in late September in Palm Beach Gardens, Florida, there was a good chance we could have severe thunderstorms every day. These storms were usually accompanied with a lot of lightning which compounded the problem. The announcement from Colin caught us by surprise and created a lot of animosity within our group.

We knew we had to bring Jack Nicklaus, our captain, and Tony Jacklin, the Captain of the European Team, into the discussion. Also in the meeting were Mark Kizziar, the President of the PGA, Mickey Powell, the Secretary of the PGA, J.R. Carpenter, the PGA Treasurer, Lou King our Executive Director, and myself, the Honorary President and Tournament Chairman.

1983 Ryder Cup Captains - Tony Jacklin and Jack Nicklaus

Attending for the Europeans were Lord Derby, the President of the British PGA, and Colin Snape, their Executive Director. After we explained the problem to everyone present, the Europeans said that they could not afford to pay for another day of charter fee if the matches were delayed. We let the captains speak. Tony did not have a lot to say. He apparently already knew the situation. When Jack was asked for his thoughts, he said if we were not going to play to a conclusion he would not bring his team out of the locker room on Friday morning. After Jack's remarks the Europeans said they would stay and play regardless.

Nicklaus' final shock of the week happened as the matches proceeded to a conclusion. The matches were the closest they had been in years and reached a point where the American side was in a position where we could lose. With the matches tied after two rounds 8-8, and again tied after ten singles matches on Sunday afternoon, Lanny Watkins was one down to J.M. Canizares playing the final hole, and Tom Watson's match was still in doubt playing the 17th hole.

If Watkins was to lose and Watson lose or tie, the Americans would lose the Ryder Cup for the first time on American soil.

Nicklaus was following the Watkins match and standing beside Watkins as he played his third shot to the 18th green. Lanny hit his 60 yard third shot to within a foot of the hole to halve his match with Canizares. Nicklaus picked up Watkins divot and kissed it. Watson won his match on the 17th hole, 2-1 over Bernard Gallacher, and the United States won the Ryder Cup 14½-13½.

For someone who thought his biggest chore as captain was to keep the players supplied with band aids and ice water, he certainly had an exciting and eventful week.

Nicklaus asked to be captain again in 1987 and to host the matches at his Muirfield Village Golf Club, in Dublin, Ohio. Unfortunately, Jack would be the first Captain to lose the Ryder Cup on American soil.

## President Reagan and the Ryder Cup

I was Chairman of the 1983 Ryder Cup Matches played at PGA National Golf Club in Palm Beach Gardens, Florida. Jack Nicklaus was selected Captain of the American Team and Tony Jacklin was Captain of the European Team. The Opening and Closing Ceremonies are quite elaborate affairs at these matches. At the Opening Ceremony, both teams and their respective officials march in, led by bagpipers, and are seated on a raised stage. There are comments made by the Presidents of the respective organizations. The Captains are introduced, make any comments they wish to make, and then introduce their respective teams.

The American flag is raised while the national anthem is being played, followed by the raising of the flags of each country represented while that country's national anthem is being played. The draw for the first round matches is announced and the teams are led off of the stage by the bagpipers. The closing ceremonies are essentially the same except the Ryder Cup is presented to the winning Captain.

In our planning sessions, we thought it would be a great idea for President Ronald Reagan to call the winning Captain to congratulate him and his team during the closing ceremony. We were able to arrange this with the White House and had a special telephone line installed to be used to receive this one call from the President.

At the conclusion of the matches, which were won by United States Team, in one of the closest matches ever, by a score of 14½ to 13½, the teams and officials were lining up to be led onto the stage when the phone at the podium rang. Mark Kizziar, the President of the PGA of America, was going to answer the phone, speak to the President, and hand it to Jack Nicklaus to talk to the President. When the phone started ringing, Mark ran to the stage yelling, "Get Jack to the stage."

Mark picked up the phone and introduced himself and said, "How are you Mr. President."

The response on the other end of the line was, "Who is this?"

"Mark Kizziar, who is this?"

The voice on the other end said, "This is the cart barn."

So much for a dedicated line to receive only one call from the President of the United States. As fate would have it, the President was not able to make the call. He had to call a special meeting of the National Security Council because of the crisis in Lebanon.

## Verde Dickey, Securing My Future

Verde Dickey is one of my best and longest friends. We met at the Oak Cliff Country Club in Dallas, not too long after I started working on the tour. Through Earl Stewart, Jr., the golf professional at Oak Cliff, I was made an honorary

149

member of the club. Since Oak Cliff was the host club for the Dallas Open, it was great for me and the club. I only lived a couple of miles from the club, so when I was home from the tour, I would play golf at the club. Verde was also a member at Oak Cliff and I met him when we played golf together one day.

We hit it off right from the start. We continued to play together when we could. At the time, he was a home builder with another Oak Cliff member, Bill Page. Verde was a graduate of Southern Methodist University and played on the SMU baseball team. He was drafted by the Cleveland Indians Baseball Club and was assigned to Pampa, of the West Texas New Mexico League. Unfortunately, his career was interrupted by the Korean War. After returning from service in Korea, he realized that he was not likely to make it to the big leagues, so he decided to pursue a business career.

Verde was just taking up golf, so when we played, I would help him with his game. He was a golf addict! Because of the type of business he was in, he could spend a good deal of time at the golf course. With his ample athletic abilities, his skill level progressed very quickly. It was not long before he was shooting in the 80's. We were playing the Sahara Invitational Tournament in the fall, and the sponsor needed more players for the pro-amateur. I asked Verde if he would like to play. This cemented our relationship and began his interest in my professional career.

It was not long after this that Verde and Bill Page decided to sever their relationship. Verde sold his interest in their business to Page. After researching several business opportunities, he decided to start a steel deck manufacturing company in Phoenix. He chose Phoenix because he thought it would be a better place to raise his family than California. His deck company was going to be the first such company west of Dallas. He felt like he would have a competitive advantage over companies in Dallas or other eastern cities because his freight rates would be considerably less than his competitors.

After Verde moved to Phoenix, he would continue to come to Dallas for lessons and to play a little golf. Also, he would invite me to come to Phoenix. Over the years, our time together developed into a very close relationship. Verde began to talk to me about going into business for myself. He knew that even though I had a very good position at Brookhaven and with CCA, I would not be able to create real wealth while I was with Bob Dedman. He felt the only way to do that was as an entrepreneur. We had discussions about my capabilities and what kind of business best fit my skills. Obviously, it had to be in the field of golf. We finally decided that I had the ability to start a golf course development and management company.

From my years with Bob Dedman, I had a great deal of exposure to all phases of club operations. CCA was built on the mistakes of developers who used the golf course component of a real estate development as a loss leader. After the developer sold out his real estate, we would acquire his club. Through good management practices and marketing, we could turn these loss leaders into profit centers for CCA. My business idea was to become a consultant to the developer during the planning and construction of the golf facility and then manage the facility for the owner after the facility was open. I felt, with my knowledge and expertise, and with my ability to attract top flight people in the industry, we could create profit centers for the developers instead of loss leaders. This proved to be a very valid and profitable business strategy.

With this strategy as a basis for the business, we decided I would start a new golf development and management company which we named Western Golf Properties. The business arrangement was that Verde would put up the capital for the company and he and I would split all profits. As an employee of the company, I would receive a substantial salary as well as the fringe benefits that he and I agreed to. I was free to run the company as I saw fit with no interference from Verde. He had his own company to run anyway. Western Golf Properties was formed January 1, 1985. I spent exactly twenty years at Brookhaven and CCA.

During my seventeen years as President of Western Golf Properties, we worked on seventy-five Real Estate Golf Course Developments for some of the finest companies and developers in the country. During these seventeen years, Verde and I had a lot of fun and did a lot of traveling together. We became like brothers in our relationship. The reason Verde wanted to do this was to create wealth for me. He felt that for all of my contributions to the game of golf I deserved more than I was going to achieve at Brookhaven and with CCA. We had a great run and worked with some of finest people in the industry.

## My MacGregor Driver

One of the things I was able to achieve while I was President of the PGA was to expand the Board of Directors to include two Independent businessmen to be selected by the President. I felt that the Board would benefit from having a couple of people who could give us a different perspective about the Association than we would get from an all golf professional Board. These independent directors would serve a three year term. The first person invited to join the Board was my good friend Verde Dickey. Verde was an outstanding businessman and had been a partner in a very successful home building business and then formed Verco Manufacturing Company, which manufactured steel decking used in the construction of the major high rise facilities in the country. To me, Verde was the consummate entrepreneur and at that time most of the golf professionals in the country were entrepreneurs. I thought he would be a good fit with our Board.

With Verde joining the Board of Directors it gave us the opportunity to spend quite a bit more time together. During his time on the Board he would come to Dallas to play golf and have me work on his golf game. This was the era before metal wood clubs. At that time most of the clubs were made with wood from persimmon trees. One of the more popular models was manufactured by MacGregor Golf Company and endorsed by Tommy Armour.

I had played with the Tommy Armour woods for several years and had a spare driver in the event I broke my primary driver. When Verde would visit, he would always look at my clubs and fell in love with my spare driver. He tried to get me to give it to him, but I refused because persimmon headed clubs would break occasionally and I knew I could

play about as well with my back up driver as I could with my primary club.

On one of his trips to Dallas, he placed my back up driver in his bag and made a big show of planning to take it home with him. He finally did take it after one trip and I

Verde Dickey making a presentation to Joe

had to steal it back on my next trip to Phoenix. This friendly effort by Verde to acquire my driver took on a life of its own, with me inspecting his golf bag prior to his returning home after each visit.

When a PGA President completes his term of office there is a dinner during the annual business meeting to thank him for his service to the association. This dinner is attended by all of the delegates and their spouses as well as other people in the industry. It is quite an elaborate affair with a lot of speeches and some excellent entertainment. There is an appropriate gift presented to the President to thank him for

153

his years of service. During my President's dinner, it was announced that Verde had contributed $50,000 to the PGA Hall of Fame in my name. This was a complete surprise and meant a great deal to me.

I had a suite in the Hyatt Reunion Tower hotel in Dallas where the meeting was being conducted and I invited Verde and a few other good friends to my suite for a party at the conclusion of the meeting. During the party I asked for everyone's attention and presented Verde with my backup driver as a gift of appreciation for his friendship and the contribution to the PGA Hall of Fame.

## Significant Events in Golf 1980-1989

**The American Junior Golf Association:** Mike Bentley, a golf writer from DeKalb County, Georgia, realized the need for a national organization dedicated to providing golf tournaments open to junior golfers who aspire to play golf at the college level. These tournaments would provide a stage for them to showcase their talents to college golf coaches who make the scholarship decisions for their university golf teams. The AJGA would conduct tournaments across the country giving junior golfers access to their tournaments. This organization was formed as a membership organization and only the top juniors in the country would be invited to join.

The AJGA now has approximately five thousand members and conducts about eighty-five tournaments a year for these junior golfers. The organization is funded by corporate sponsors both from within and outside the golf industry. Graduates from the AJGA also are very active in providing funds. Most of the players on the PGA and LPGA tour who participated in AJGA tournaments contribute to the AJGA fund with a percentage of their winnings.

Some of the leading players on the PGA Tour who are graduates of the AJGA are: Tiger Woods, Phil Mickelson,

Jim Furyk, Sergio Garcia, Matt Kuchar, Dustin Johnson, Justin Leonard, Hunter Mahan, Sean O'Hair, David Toms, Bubba Watson, and Scott Verplank. On the LPGA tour are Lorena Ochoa, Christie Kerr, Paula Creamer, Morgan Pressel, and Pat Hurst.

**Fitness Trailers:** When I went on the tour there was one player who had a reputation for working on his physical conditioning. That player was Frank Stranahan who was a weight lifter. Frank carried a set of bar bells with him and worked out in his hotel room. It was fun to see Frank check into his hotel. The bellman would come out to his car to get his luggage and would go to his knees when he tried to pick up the suitcase which contained the bar bells.

When Gary Player came on the tour in the early 1960's, he was a big advocate of physical fitness as well as following a very nutritional diet. Because of the great amount of time it took to fly from South Africa to the United States, Gary would regularly do pushups in the aisle of the plane as well as run in place. As Gary became more successful he always gave a part of his success to his physical condition. It did not take long for other players to begin to buy into the conditioning regimen. Deane Beman brought a proposal to the Tour Policy Board from one of the leading hospital groups to provide a fitness trailer to travel with the tour. The trailer would be staffed by a trained physical therapist who would travel with the tour and work with the players to develop a workout regimen. They would be available to help players who had minor injuries to rehab those injuries.

It did not take long for most of the players to buy into the program. When Tiger Woods joined the tour he was a big advocate of conditioning. He has a complete workout room in his home and a conditioning coach that works with him on a regular basis. Many of the other professionals have conditioning coaches that work with them regularly. Most of the players on the tour visit the fitness trailer almost every day when they are on the tour. The players today look for any way to improve their chances of being successful on the tour.

**Equipment Trailers:** When I played the tour in the 1950's, some of the companies had representatives on the tour that were responsible for tour staff. They also were scouting the new young players coming on the tour to see if they would be good additions to their staff. These representatives did not travel with the tour but showed up from time to time to take care of their staff players. If the players needed something from the company in the intervals when the representative was not on the tour everything was handled by telephone.

The staff players were asked to help with equipment development so it was not unusual for players to try new club models or new ball technology during the competitions or in the practice rounds. If a player broke a club or wanted a club loft or lie changed, it was usually done by the local club professional or a local club repair shop in the area. There were many drawbacks to this system. A lot of club professionals were not proficient in club repair. Most of them did not have the inventory of repair components of the many different club companies to be able to do a satisfactory repair job.

Over time, the manufacturers realized they had to provide better support for their staff players. Also, as new technology came into club making, it was not realistic to expect the club professionals to be able to either carry the inventory or keep up with the fast evolving change in club manufacturing. This brought about the evolution of companies developing their own club repair trailers with factory trained repair technicians and an inventory of components that allowed those technicians to do any repair or even build replacement clubs for their players. The result is that the players have been able to try clubs with different specifications and different components. They now have the best fitting equipment they have ever played with and the ability to make changes if they feel the need.

**Clubs for Kids:** When Don Padgett was President of the PGA in 1977-78, one of his primary initiatives was the formation of the PGA Junior Golf Foundation. This was formed as a non-profit foundation with the purpose to generate tax deductible contributions to be used by the PGA to promote junior golf in America. We then developed the Grand Slam of Golf which is the winners of the four major championships playing an 18 hole exhibition and attend a dinner each year with the proceeds going to the Junior Golf Foundation.

When I became President in 1981, I introduced a program that had a two-fold purpose. The program was called Clubs for Kids. The purpose was getting golf clubs in the hands of kids, particularly inner city kids. It also had the purpose of helping the club professional bring business back to the golf shop. The discount golf shops that were becoming very popular around the country were taking a lot of business out of the golf shop.

We developed a program that would give the amateur golfer the opportunity to donate his used clubs to the PGA Junior Golf foundation by turning them in to his PGA professional. The golf professional would give him a receipt with an appraised value of the clubs if he bought a new set of clubs from the professional. The professional would turn in the clubs to his local PGA Section who would put on Clubs for Kids clinics in their area and give each kid who attended some clubs and a golf lesson.

When there was a tour tournament in a community the club professionals would team with the tournament sponsors and the touring professional and have a Clubs for Kids clinic at the tournament. The clinic would be held on Tuesday afternoon and the kids would be given free admission.

The touring professionals would give the clinic. The club professionals would then give the kids free lessons and some of the golf clubs collected.

The program had a lot of success early and did create a lot of business for golf professionals as well as provide clubs for a lot of kids who had never been introduced to the game. It was also a big hit at the tour tournaments. The tour professionals enjoyed interacting with the kids and there was a lot of public relations value for the sponsors. The big negative to the program was after we had gotten the clubs in the hands of the kids they had no access to golf courses to pursue their interest.

**Yardage Books:** Starting in the 1940's, a few players would step off yardages from designated spots on the golf course to determine the yardage for a shot. Gene Andrews, a prominent amateur, is given credit for starting this practice. When Jack Nicklaus joined the tour in 1962 he used this practice extensively. More and more players began to step off the course during the practice rounds so they could use this information to determine their yardage during the playing of the tournament. Eventually the players had their caddies walk the course and develop the yardage for them. At the same time more players were having their caddies go around the course early in the morning and record the locations of the hole placements each day.

From this practice we had the evolution of the yardage book. The first yardage books were very crude, hand drawn by the caddies. From this crude start evolved more sophisticated books which showed the bunkers and other prominent features on the course. Soon the caddies carried measuring wheels with them and walked the course with these wheels to determine the precise yardage from every key feature on the course. Finally the PGA tour staff began to provide a pin location sheet to the players for each round in order to keep all of the caddies who were walking the course to chart the pin placements off the greens. With the development of the GPS measuring system the players switched from the yardage wheels to the GPS system.

Finally one of the caddies named George Lucas, who had developed a reputation of creating the best yardage book each week, decided to see if he could provide the player with his book for a fee. He then expanded his service and contracted to the tournament sponsors to provide books to them to be given to the players when they registered for the tournament. It didn't take long for the average golfer to want a yardage book at his home course. Thus a new industry was born. There are several companies that provide yardage books for golf courses.

**Electronic Scoreboard:**  The 1980's brought another new innovation that greatly improved the experience for golf fans - the electronic scoreboard. First is the ease with which the scoreboard could be installed. They were mounted on a trailer and could be pulled into place very easily or even moved if the location did not work out. Their electrical source was provided by a golf car connection made between the scoreboard and the battery of the golf car.

The scoreboard worked like a typewriter with the desired text typed into the system and it appeared instantly on the scoreboard. This gave the tournament sponsor the ability to show the leaders on scoreboards around the course. The scoreboards could be updated instantly with what was happening on the course. There was the ability to put messages on the boards with pertinent information the tour wanted to convey to the gallery. One of the most helpful uses was the ability to put weather warnings on the scoreboards around the course. The other real benefit of the electronic scoreboards is that there was not the need to have several volunteers at each location to operate the board.

**PGA Membership for Women:**  The 1980's brought about another big change in the membership eligibility of the PGA. For the first time women could become members of the PGA of America. Previously the organization was for men only. There was a feeling within the PGA that women had their own organization the Ladies Professional Golfers' Association. However the LPGA was formed as a player's organization. When it was established, there were not many women professionals in the game. Those who wanted to make their living out of golf were usually teachers of the game. The LPGA did not have the educational programs in place to train women to reach the highest levels of the profession.  As it became more apparent that women deserved the same opportunity as men, the PGA finally welcomed them into the organization.

# Decade of the 90's

## HSU Hall of Fame

In 1990, I received word from Jeff Goodin, the golf coach at Hardin-Simmons University, that I had been elected to the HSU Athletic Hall of Fame. The call took me by surprise because I had felt that I probably never would be considered. Even though we had two very successful years my first two years in school, I thought that because I had turned professional after my sophomore year, induction would never happen.

I had always been very proud of our teams' accomplishments the two years I played. As a freshman, we won the Border Conference Championship and finished second in the NAIA Championship. There were three seniors, Billy Phillips, George Smith, and Carl Chambers, and three freshmen, Tommy Hale, Jackie Clark, and me. The following year we had three sophomores and one freshman. Tommy, Jackie, and I were joined by Arlyn Scott, a freshman from Odessa. Tommy Hale won the individual honors and I finished fifth. We were named to the All-American Team.

Hardin Simmons University - 1953 NAIA Champions

I left the team with a lot of sadness, but when the opportunity was offered me to become the assistant golf professional at Abilene Country Club, it fulfilled my lifetime dream. It also gave me the opportunity to continue my education at HSU by taking night courses and some early morning classes.

The thrill of the induction ceremony was threefold for me. First, my family was able to be there for the dinner. Second, Bill Scott, the former basketball coach who also subbed as golf coach when Bill Ledbetter could not accompany the team, accepted my invitation to formally do the induction. The third thrill was that Clyde "Bulldog" Turner and Sammy Baugh attended the dinner.

I got to know Sammy while I was living in Abilene and he was on the coaching staff at Hardin-Simmons. I met Bulldog in Bill Ledbetter's office when he came back in the off season from Chicago. After I went on the tour, Bulldog would always come out to the golf course to watch me play when I played in Chicago. After I moved to Dallas he would stop by Brookhaven to visit when he was in Dallas.

Bill Scott and I became friends when I was in school. We had an immediate connection because his wife Billy was from Lamesa and her dad Bill White had a big influence on my life while I was growing up. He made it possible for me to attend Hardin-Simmons. Of course, Bill became General Willie Scott, the commanding general of the Texas National Guard.

Starting in 1990, Jeff Goodin asked me to lend my name to a golf tournament to raise money for the golf team. I am proud to say we have celebrated the 20th anniversary of the Joe Black Golf Classic.

## Forty-Eight Years at The Masters

I was first invited to attend The Masters Tournament as a rules official in 1959. Little did I know it would become a 48 year journey. The invitation came from Cliff Roberts, who with Bobby Jones, founded the Augusta National Golf Club. At that time, the Rules Committee Chairman was a member of the club by the name of Frank Edwards. Mr. Edwards did not present himself as a rules expert, but he was simply the facilitator. He made the rules assignments for the committee members and conducted the Rules Committee Meetings during the tournament. If there were any major problems during the tournament, Mr. Roberts would be consulted before a decision was made.

The Rules Committee at that time was comprised of Harold Sargent, who was a Past President of The PGA of America and the Golf Professional at East Lake Country Club (the Club in Atlanta where Bob Jones was a member and where he learned his golf as a young boy); Jack Sargent, Harold's brother who was the Golf Professional at Peach Tree Country Club in Atlanta; Warren Orlick, another Past President of the PGA of America who was Golf Professional at Tam O'Shanter Country Club in Detroit, Michigan; Harvey Raynor, the PGA Tour Director; myself, and a few other members of the club.

A couple of members of the committee were USGA Executive Committee members as well as members of Augusta National. Each of us was assigned areas of the course to be responsible for any rules problems. A couple of the USGA Executive Committee Members were assigned as rovers. Their responsibility was to ride around their assigned area in a golf cart and assist any of the Rules Committee Members who may need help with a rules situation.

There were a few places on the golf course that were particularly difficult as far as the rules of golf were concerned. These holes were assigned to the members of the committee who were considered the rules experts. I always knew that I would be working these holes during the tournament. The problem areas were Holes 11, 12, 13, 15, and 16.

As time went on, it became obvious to Cliff Roberts that the make-up of the Masters Rules Committee had to change. The tournament was too significant to have the Committee comprised of people who were not qualified to administer the rules of golf. The make-up of the Committee was changed to include members of the USGA Executive Committee who were qualified to administer the rules of golf, as well as the Executive Director of the USGA, and the President, Secretary, and Treasurer of the PGA of America – all who were golf professionals. Other committee members included the Secretary of the R&A Golf Club who conducted the play of the British Open, the Chairman of the R&A Rules Committee, and other experts from golf associations around the world.

My responsibilities changed dramatically after the 1968 Masters Tournament. Until that time, the members of the club handled the scoring responsibilities at the 9th and 18th greens. They simply placed a round umbrella table behind the green with four lawn chairs. A couple of members would sit at the table and greet each player after they finished their round. The players would check their scorecard and hand it to the members.

The fallacy of this scoring procedure was exposed when Roberto DeVicenzo returned a wrong scorecard in the final round of the tournament in 1968. When DeVicenzo finished his round, it was thought that he and Bob Goalby had tied for the tournament lead and that a play-off would be required the next day to determine the winner. However, a player's score is not official until the player has checked his hole by hole score and signed his scorecard verifying them to be correct.

Unfortunately, Tommy Aaron, DeVicenzo's scorer, had recorded a four for the 17th hole when he had made a three. When Roberto arrived at the scorer's table, which was placed near the ropes behind the 18th green, the gallery was trying to talk to him and get his autograph. Roberto became distracted with all the commotion and missed the four which Aaron had recorded for his score at the 17th hole. He returned his card to the committee and left the table.

The score he signed for was in fact one shot higher than his actual score. However, the score had to stand because if a player signs for a score higher than he actually made, the score stands. If it had been a lower score than the actual score he made he would have been disqualified. However, it did cost him the opportunity to have a playoff with Bob Goalby for the Masters title.

That winter I received a call from Cliff Roberts telling me he had a special assignment for me. He said they were going to put a tent behind the 18th green under the television tower and would like for me to assume the responsibility of handling the scoring at the 18th hole after the players finished their round. I would also be responsible for the rules on both the 9th and 18th holes. I told Cliff that I would prefer to continue to work on the course, that I enjoyed that very much.

He told me, "Joe Ed" (he always called me Joe Ed), I would consider it a personal favor if you did this for me."

That ended the argument. I must say I did enjoy the experience for the next 38 years. I probably would not have been invited back for all of those years without that assignment – and would not have had the opportunity to interact with the players as much. For all those years, I was always the first one to greet the new champion when the tournament was over.

## The Greatest Players

I have seen a lot of great players over the years. Obviously Arnold Palmer was the greatest player while I was running the PGA tour. Jack Nicklaus had only played three years when I left that position. I think Jack Nicklaus is the greatest player to date. Obviously what Tiger Woods is doing now is setting new standards. But Ben Hogan was so Hogan. He was so good as a ball striker that it was unbelievable. The most impactful player before Tiger was Arnold Palmer. He was very charismatic and he lifted the game to a new level. He brought so many people into the game who were non-golfers. Tiger Woods is doing that today.

Jack was a phenomenal player. But Arnold did more spectacular things: pitching the ball in, chipping the ball in, holing long putts, etc. And Tiger does the same things today. If you are going to have a player play the 18th hole for you, the only one to do it is Tiger. Just like a recent tournament, Tiger started the day 2 over for the first three holes and ended up 6 under. As Tiger was playing the 18th hole, the commentator Nick Faldo, said, "You know he'll make an eagle here."

Sure enough, Tiger knocked the ball in from 8 feet and made an eagle. He's phenomenal that way. But all the great athletes are!

## Significant Events in Golf 1990-1999

**Tiger Woods** is without a doubt the most significant occurrence of the 1990's. He came on the tour with a lot of anticipation and certainly did not disappoint. Tiger's legacy cannot finally be written for several years yet but most people feel he is the greatest player to ever play the game. People measure greatness in many different ways but the gold standard seems to be by the number of major championships won. Jack Nicklaus has won a record 18 Major Championships during his career and 73 total wins, second only to Sam Snead's 82 total victories. Woods has won 14 Major Championships and 71 total victories. Nicklaus won his last Major Championship, the Masters Tournament, in 1986 at age 46 and Woods is only 34 years of age. However no one has dominated the game the way Woods has for the time he has played.

**Golf Channel:** When Golf Channel was founded in 1995 there were a lot of people who doubted it would succeed. I was among those who had doubts. It did not seem possible that a 24 hour a day television programing of golf could survive. Golf tournaments and teaching programs had to be the bulk of the content but there were only so many golf tournaments and so many teachers of the game.

Even then they did not have access to a lot of the tournaments due to their rights being owned by the major television networks. Being a cable network did give Golf Channel the ability to market itself to golf subscribers through existing cable networks. Today with millions of subscribers and the innovative way they have been able to find a niche in live and delayed broadcasting of golf tournaments and creating other interesting golf programming that has been well received, they have become a permanent fixture in golf.

**Judy Bell USGA President:**  The 1990's brought about the opportunities for more women in the game. Judy Bell had a great career as a player. She played on the 1960 and 1962 United States Curtis Cup Team. She also served as a volunteer to the USGA for many years beginning in 1961 as a member of the Junior Golf Committee. She later served on the Women's Committee of the USGA. She became the first woman elected to the Board of Directors in 1987. Judy was honored for her tremendous contribution to the USGA and to golf by being elected the USGA President in 1996, the first woman to be so honored. Judy did a great job as president of the USGA and opened the door for other women to serve in similar capacities in other golf and sports organizations. Judy was elected to the World Golf Hall of Fame in 2001.

**Environmental Institute for Golf:**  For many years the Golf Course Superintendent's Association had the GCSAA Foundation which solicited contributions from their members and friends as well as from people in the golf industry who did business with the golf courses of the country and their superintendents. Some of the contributions were for specific purposes and some were unrestricted. The contributions were primarily for two purposes, either to provide scholarships for high school graduates who wanted to pursue a career in the turf industry or to provide the funds for turf research.

The foundation raised a fair amount of money for these purposes but the 1990's brought about an attack on the golf industry. These attacks were from the environmental community who felt that golf course maintenance practices were a detriment to the environment. Even though those in the industry disagreed with this assessment it was felt there was not enough research available to support the position of the industry. The Foundation was not generating enough contributions to expand the research efforts to support the industry claims.

The foundation was administered by the GCSAA staff and the governing Board of Directors was essentially insiders. The decision was made to expand the Board of Directors of the Foundation to bring in other interested parties, whether they were individuals or Organizations. The purpose of this change was to expand the reach of the Foundation. I was asked to serve on the Foundation Board because I was President of Western Golf Properties and a former President of the PGA of America. My company also had made a substantial contribution to the GCSAA Foundation. The new Board included current players on the PGA and Senior PGA tours, Golf Course Architects, Representatives from the PGA Tour, the USGA, the PGA of America and the American Society of Golf Course Architects as well as Golf Course Owners and other interested parties.

After a period of time it was felt if the Foundation was going to achieve its goal of attracting more money and more awareness of the efforts of the Foundation, there needed to be a name change and a new mission statement. Herb Kohler the Chairman of The Kohler Company and owner of The American Club and the two golf courses at Whistling Straits and the two courses at Black Wolf Run, was the one who suggested The Environmental Institute for Golf as the new name for the Foundation.

Because of this new name and the ability to generate more money because the new makeup of the Board and with the efforts of such people as Greg Norman who came on the Board and headed up the fund raising efforts, there has been a significant increase in the amount of research being done to change and improve the maintenance practices of the industry. I truly enjoyed the five years I served on the Board and am particularly proud to have been the Chairman when we changed the name.

**Junior Golf:** There were several significant things happen in junior golf that impacted the game. First and foremost was the development of The First Tee Program. The First Tee was founded in 1997 by the World Golf Foundation. The Founding partners were The PGA of America, The PGA Tour, The United States Golf Association, The Ladies Professional Golf Association, and The Masters Tournament. The Mission Statement adopted was to impact the lives of young people by providing learning facilities and educational programs that promote character development and life-enhancing values through the game of golf. The life skills developed and taught at the First Tee facilities around the country are Responsibility, Respect, Confidence, Sportsmanship, Judgment, Honesty, Integrity, Perseverance, and Courtesy. Though the First Tee is open to all income levels the focus is to attract inner city kids.

Today there are two hundred and one independent chapters in 50 states as well as six international locations, over 3.5 million participants and over eleven hundred affiliated golf courses that offer participants free or reduced fees access. The program is run by approximately 8,500 volunteers that include coaches, PGA and LPGA and touring professionals.

**Junior Golf Clubs** are another reason that golf has seen a strong upswing in participation. Until the 1990s when junior golfers were introduced to the game, they were usually supplied with adult clubs which had been cut off to reduce the length. Length is only one of many factors that are taken into consideration when fitting a person with golf clubs. The other things to be considered include weight, the flexibility of the shaft, the size of the grip, and the lie of the club. In 1997 U.S. Kids Golf was established to manufacturer clubs specifically designed for kids. Butch Baird a former touring professional was also very involved in the manufacturing of kids clubs. With clubs that were specifically designed for kids it made it a lot easier to learn and play the game.

**PGA Junior Golf Tours:** The American Junior Golf Association was founded to provide the premier juniors who were hoping to secure a golf scholarship a place to showcase their talents. The AJGA did not satisfy the need for tournament opportunities for the other millions of junior golfers who would like to enjoy competition but did not have the skills to participate at the highest level.

The forty one PGA Sections accepted the challenge of conducting junior tours in their areas. These tours run for several weeks with one or two tournaments a week. These have been very successful and create the opportunity to teach the rules and etiquette of the game as well as provide competition for the kids. Most of these tours require the kids to attend classes on rules and the etiquette of the game as well as care of the golf course and the code of conduct. There are thousands who participate on these tours each summer. The state golf associations also conduct such tours for their member clubs.

**Golf Academies:** Some of the leading golf instructors have developed Junior Golf Academies where kids can enroll and receive intense instruction for many months or even years. These have proved to be very successful with a lot of the top juniors in the country having developed their games at these academies. There have even been parents who have moved their families across the country just so their kid can take advantage of these opportunities. Two of the most successful junior golf academies are conducted by Hank Haney and David Ledbetter.

# Decade of the 2000's

## First Tee of Phoenix

One of the projects that I was involved with when I retired as President of Western Golf Properties was the construction of The First Tee of Phoenix golf course. The project was a joint venture between The Thunderbirds Organization, the sponsors of The Phoenix Open golf tournament, and Luther Alkasea, who owned The Thunderbird Golf Course. It was a public golf course which was very much in need of renovation. The plan was to renovate the existing course and build a 9-hole short course to be used by the kids in the First Tee program, which was run by the Thunderbirds organization. The public golf course would be run as a for profit facility with the profits to be used to pay for the operation of the First Tee Course. It was a coincidence that the Thunderbird name was in fact the name of the course as well as the Phoenix Open sponsor.

First Tee sculpture in Phoenix

When I was contacted by the Thunderbird Organization about our involvement in the project, I agreed to contribute fifty percent of our fee to the project. As we got into the planning process, I offered to talk to Tom Fazio, one of the premier golf course designers, to design the course for no fee. Our company had worked with the Fazio Organizations on several projects and the experience had been very good

173

for both of us. We were just finishing up the construction of The Meadows Del Mar Golf Course in Del Mar, California, with Tom Fazio as the Designer and Western Golf as the construction manager and we also would manage the course for the owner. At the dedication ceremony for the Meadows Del Mar Golf Course I ask Tom about designing the First Tee Course and he readily agreed.

I stepped down as the President of Western Golf Properties just as we were finishing the construction of the First Tee Course. We appointed Hugh Edgmon, one of our executives, as President of the company and Hugh began working with the Thunderbirds on the First Tee project. After I resigned as President, we decided to move home to Texas. We bought 30 acres in Dripping Springs and developed a little ranch. We began the construction of a house and began fencing the property, clearing the cedar trees, and planting grasses. I was having a lot of fun.

One day I received a call from Hugh Edgmon telling me the First Tee course was ready to open and the Thunderbirds were planning a huge opening ceremony and would like for me to attend. I told him I could not because the Joe Black Cup Matches were being played on the same day. The matches were being played at the Comanche Trace Golf Club in Kerrville, Texas. I told him he was now President of Western Golf so he should be the one representing the company.

A couple of days later Hugh called me again and told me that Tim Finchem the Commissioner of the PGA Tour, Joe Louis Barrow the Executive Director of the National First Tee Organization, former Vice President Dan Quyale, as well as the Mayor of the City of Phoenix would be attending and they would very much like me to attend. I told Hugh again I could not attend that I had to make some remarks at the Sunday night dinner of the Joe Black Cup Matches and be at the opening on Monday morning. I also told him we had a barbeque by the Pedernales River Monday evening with Jerry Jeff Walker entertaining and I did not feel I should miss any of the functions.

A few days later Hugh called again and told me that I had to attend. He said the Thunderbirds were placing a sculpture in front of the First Tee Clubhouse that I had recommended to them. And that they were going to dedicate it to Tom Fazio, Luther Alkasea, and me. They wanted the dedication of the sculpture to be a surprise. I then told Hugh I would come if I could make the proper arrangements. I managed to get an early flight out of Austin. Hugh picked me up and drove me to the Thunderbird Golf Course for the Opening Ceremony. After the Ceremony there was a luncheon and I caught a flight back to Austin and drove the two hours to Kerrville and made it in time for the barbeque.

I am glad I went back for the dedication ceremony. It is quite an honor to have a sculpture in front of the Phoenix First Tee clubhouse dedicated to you.

## Texas Golf Hall of Fame

When I returned to Texas from Arizona, where I had lived for 18 years, I learned that the Texas Golf Hall of Fame had been abandoned in 1997. I had lost track of a lot of things happening in Texas golf.

The Hall of Fame was started in 1978 at the Texas National Golf Club in Willis, Texas. Bob Payne, the Director of Golf at Texas National, was the person who convinced the developers of the club that the Hall of Fame would be a great amenity for their development and would help with real estate and membership sales at the club. The first inductees into the Hall were Ben Hogan, Byron Nelson, Jimmy Demaret, David "Spec" Goldman, Lee Trevino, Hardy Loudermilk, and the great Mildred "Babe" Didrikson Zaharias.

Each year there would be a Pro-Amateur on the day of the induction ceremony, with a dinner that evening when the inductees would be enshrined into the Hall of Fame. At that time, a large picture of them would be hung on the wall of the club house. I was inducted into the Hall of Fame in 1982, along with Jay Hebert, Billy Maxwell, Kathy Whitworth, Bill Rogers, and Dave Williams, the long time University of Houston golf coach.

Texas National sold the Hall of Fame to The Woodlands development, which paid $50,000.00 for the corporate entity as well as all of the artifacts. The Hall of Fame was relocated to the TPC Golf Course at The Woodlands. It had its own facility, which provided the opportunity to properly display the pictures of the Hall of Fame members. There was also space for displays of artifacts and memorabilia to enhance the experience for those attending the Hall of Fame. It was a great attraction during the Shell Houston Open. Many attending the golf tournament took the opportunity to stop by and visit the Hall of Fame. The media center was also located next door to the Hall of Fame, so a lot of the media would take the opportunity to visit.

When The Woodlands Corporation bought the Hall of Fame, they got the Houston Golf Association to assume the responsibility of operating the Hall. Duke Butler, the Executive Director of the HGA, became the CEO of the Hall, and Bert Darden, the HGA Publicity Director, was also asked to help. Frances Trimble was employed as the Executive Director. The Woodlands Corporation and the HGA operated the Hall of Fame for several years with Frances Trimble handling the day to day operations and The Woodlands Corporation funding any operating losses.

The reason the Hall of Fame was closed is that The Woodlands Corporation was negotiating to sell The Woodlands Development and the buyers did not want to continue its operation. The Woodlands Corporation had all of the memorabilia and artifacts, as well as all of the pictures, packed and put into storage. The Woodlands Corporation made an agreement to donate the Hall of Fame to the HGA with the understanding they would open a new Hall of

Fame at Memorial Park Golf Course located in Houston, or to another location if approved by The Woodlands Corporation. The agreement provided that if they had not found a new home for the Hall of Fame within one year, everything would be returned to The Woodlands.

The HGA tried, without success, to make arrangements to locate the Hall of Fame at Memorial Park as well as several other locations. During this time, the donated golf clubs and several boxes of the other memorabilia were removed from storage. The best information is that they were used to set up displays for potential interested parties to try to convince them to become the new home of the Hall of Fame. I was told they were taken to the HGA warehouse. Early the next year, more items were removed to set up a display during the Shell Houston Open. Again, I was told these items were taken to the HGA warehouse.

The next year, the final boxes were delivered to the HGA warehouse by Johnny Melia Storage, where the items had been stored. At some point the HGA tried to return some of the items to the people who donated them to the Hall of Fame. It was confirmed that the Hall of Fame photographs were returned to Texas National Golf Club, one of the original golf cars was returned to San Antonio Country Club, and a fresno used to build golf courses, was taken to Watson Distributing, though it had been donated by Frances Trimble. Watson is no longer in business and no one knows what happened to the fresno.

In January of 2008, I told the Northern and Southern Texas PGA's I would try to reconstitute the Hall of Fame. My thought was that the various golf associations of Texas should own the Hall of Fame. As soon as word got out that I was trying to revive the Hall of Fame, I was told I should talk to Reid Meyers at the Municipal Golf Association of San Antonio. This organization is a non-profit, formed to manage the municipal golf courses for the city. Reid had become aware that the Hall of Fame had been abandoned and had the idea of reviving it and placing it at Brackenridge Park

Golf Course in San Antonio. I contacted Reid and agreed to meet him at Brackenridge Park to talk about the Hall of Fame. As our meeting progressed it became apparent to both of us that we should join forces.

Since that time, we have brought the two PGA's of Texas, the Texas Golf Association, and the Women's Texas Golf Associations together to agree to be the owners of the Texas Golf Hall of Fame. We have received approval from the State of Texas and filed for non-profit designation from the Internal Revenue Service. We have a Board of Directors, comprised of fifteen people, with seven coming from the golf associations, two from the SAMGA, one from the Pan American Golf Association, and five at large members elected by the Board of Directors. We have signed an agreement between the Hall of Fame and the SAMGA for the location of the Hall at Brackenridge Park and the MGA to operate the Hall of Fame for the Board.

We have not been able to find most of the artifacts and memorabilia that were stored in the HGA warehouse. The HGA could only find an old greens mower, a hole cutter, a few books, and a filing cabinet with a lot of the old files. We have been able to retrieve the pictures from Texas National. Over the 10 year period, the balance of the items that were in the HGA warehouse disappeared. The HGA does not know what happened to them. This is a huge loss because most of the items donated by the Hall of Fame members are irreplaceable.

## Significant Events of Golf 2000-2009

**Tiger Slam:** Arnold Palmer was the first player to declare a goal of winning the four professional major championships in the same year. This was an outgrowth of Bobby Jones achieving his grand slam by winning the British Open and Amateur championships as well as the U.S. Open and U.S. Amateur in 1930. Several players since Palmer have tried to achieve the same goal but have not been able to successfully fulfill this ambitious undertaking.

Each year the winner of The Masters Tournament is asked by the media if that becomes their goal and to assess their chance of achieving that phenomenal feat. The only one who has really embraced the possibility is Tiger Woods. Tiger, on more than one occasion, has stated at the beginning of the year that this is his goal and he thinks it may be achievable. Tiger did not win the 1999 Masters Tournament so the grand slam became a moot point. He then proceeded to win the U.S. Open, the British Open, and the PGA Championship for one of the most phenomenal feats in golf. He then won the 2001 Masters Tournament to be the only player to ever hold all four of these titles at one time. This was truly an amazing feat and became known as the Tiger Slam.

The only other player to win three of these championships consecutively was the great Ben Hogan who won the 1953 Masters, U.S. Open, and British Open, but did not play in the PGA Championship. Ben had traveled to Britain by ship and would not return in time to compete in the PGA. He probably would not have played any way because it was doubtful he could walk the ten rounds required to win the PGA Championship which was played as match play at that time.

**The World Golf Championships:** At the 1996 Presidents Cup Matches, five world governing bodies met and formed the International Federation of PGA Tours. Those five organizations were the European Tour, Japan Golf Tour, PGA Tour, PGA Tour of Australia, and the Sunshine Tour. The Asian Tour joined the organization in 1999. The purpose of forming the organization was to develop the key elements necessary to develop new international events.

The impetus for forming the organization was the effort made by Greg Norman a couple of years before to form a world tour. Greg had the television and financing in place to start such a tour. However he would have to convince the leading players from around the world to leave their home tours and join his organization. Tim Finchem, the PGA Tour Commissioner, made it very clear that anyone joining the Norman tour would lose their right to play on the PGA Tour. As a result Norman cancelled his plans for a new world tour.

Some of the leading U.S. players for several years had expressed an interest in having more events where all of the leading players in the world could come together to test their skills against the best players in the world. At that time the only events where all of the leading players could compete against each other were the major championships.

In order to conduct the World Golf Championships, the International Federation of PGA Tours had to develop a method of qualifying to compete in the Word Golf events. With the World Golf Rankings being available to rate players by their performance in the tournaments on their respective tours and the individual tours having their ranking systems to determine qualifications from their own events, a system was developed to use both methods to determine the qualifications for the World Golf Championships.

The first event, the Accenture Match Play Championship, was played at the La Costa Resort in Carlsbad, California, in 1999. There are four World Golf Championships played each year; the Accenture Match Play Championship, the CA Championship, the Bridgestone Invitational, and the HSBC Champions. The tournaments have been played in six countries including the United States. The countries hosting these tournaments are Australia, Spain, Ireland, England and China. However the majority of the events have been conducted in the U.S.

**Olympic Golf:** In the mid 2000's, the PGA Tour, the R&A, the PGA of America, the Masters Tournament, and the LPGA began a concerted effort to have golf included as one of the Olympic sports for the 2016 Olympic Games. This was not the first time that an effort had been made to get golf included as an Olympic Sport. In fact, golf was included in the 1900 and 1904 Olympic Summer Games. In 1900 it was conducted as a women's sport and 1904 as a men's sport.

After a very well run campaign by the golf organizations and many individual players including Tiger Woods and Michelle Wie, the Olympic Committee meeting in 2009 at Copenhagen voted to include golf at the 2016 Summer Olympic Games in Brazil. The feeling in the international golf community is that this will create an explosion of interest worldwide in the game. The inclusion of golf in the Olympics coupled with the success we are seeing on the PGA and LPGA tours from international players is sure to fuel this explosion.

**FedEx Cup:**  For years there has been a real problem between the PGA tour and the tour tournament sponsors, particularly sponsors who have tournaments after the Labor Day weekend. In fact, most of the leading players played very little after the PGA Championship in mid August. There were several reasons for this. One of the more prominent reasons was the development of several specialty events such as The Skins Games, the Three Tour Challenge, the Shark Shootout, and similar events that had a limited field with all players being assured of a substantial guaranteed payday even if they finish last. There was also the opportunity for these players to go overseas and play in events on the other world tours with  appearance money being paid as well as what the player may win in the tournament.

Television did not want to televise the events after Labor Day because their ratings dropped considerably because of the absence of the top players and the competition from both college and professional football and the ending of the baseball season and the playing of the World Series.

There was also the argument that the tour did not have an ending event like all other sports. Baseball has the World Series, football has the Super Bowl, and basketball has the Final Four and the NBA Playoffs. There was no playoff and ending to the PGA Tour.

Tim Finchem, the Commissioner of the PGA Tour and his staff, set about trying to solve this problem. This brought about the FedEx Cup, which is a series of four events that the players qualify for by accumulating points from each tournament over the course of the year. Soon after the PGA Championship this point accumulation ends and the top 125 players with the most points earn the right into the first of the four FedEx Tournaments. Each of these tournaments has a regular purse the players are competing for as well as the continued accumulation of points.

After the first tournament, the top one hundred players, determined by the points accumulated, advance to the second tournament and after that event the top seventy players advance to the third event. After the third tournament the top thirty players advance to the PGA Tour Championship and the finals of the FedEx Cup.

After the third tournament the points are redistributed so any of the top five players in the final tournament will automatically win the FedEx Cup if they win the tournament. Any of the other players could possibly win the $10 Million Dollar first place money depending on how the points are distributed at the conclusion of the tournament. The FedEx Cup purse is in addition to the purse of the Tour Championship. The players are essentially playing in two tournaments at one time.

The Tour Championship and the FedEx Cup have proven to bring to an end the PGA Tour season and created lots of excitement at the end of the golf season as well as provided the vehicle to keep television interested in the tour after the PGA Championship and created better television ratings for the TV networks. There is still a series of five tournaments after the Tour Championship to provide playing opportunities for the players who want to play into the fall. These tournaments are usually played for a lesser purse than the earlier tournaments but are very important to the players competing. The tournaments count for the money list where the top 125 players earn an exemption for the following season and the winners of these events earn an exemption for the next two years. It also provides an opportunity for these players to earn substantially more money for the year.

# About the Author

Joe Black is a "doer" with a golfing career that spans four decades. It all began at Lamesa High School, continued at Hardin Simmons University in Abilene where he played on the 1953 NAIA National Championship Team. After HSU he played three years on the PGA Tour. In 1958 he became a Tournament Supervisor on the PGA Tour Staff. He built his reputation as a Rules of Golf expert during his years on the tour.

He was so knowledgeable of the Rules of Golf, he was a world-wide speaker on the subject and served as Chairman of the Rules Committee of the PGA of America and as a member of the USGA Rules Committee. He also served for 48 years on the Masters Tournament Rules Committee, the last 39 handling the rules and scoring at the 18th green.

In 1965 he became Director of Golf at the 54-hole Brookhaven Country Club, Dallas, TX as well as Vice President of golf for Club Corporation of America, which owned such prestigious clubs as Brookhaven, Firestone, and Pinehurst. Black elected Treasurer of the Northern Texas PGA from 1969-70 and President in 1971-72. He became the national Treasurer in 1977 and President of the PGA of America in 1981-82.

The annual Joe Black Cup Matches were started in 1981 by Black's peers who hold him in high esteem. The matches are played between the club professionals from the Southern Texas PGA against their Northern Texas PGA counterparts.

Black served as:

- Chairman of the PGA Rules Committee from 1969-1976.

- Chairman of the PGA Championship in 1979 and 1980

- Chairman of the PGA Senior Championship in1983

- Captain of the PGA Cup Team in 1981-1983-1984
- Chairman of the Ryder Cup Matches in 1983

Black is a member of the:

- PGA of America Hall of Fame
- Texas Golf Hall of Fame
- Hardin-Simmons University Sports Hall of Fame

In 2005 Black was selected to receive one of Hardin-Simmons University's most prestigious awards: The Hall of Leaders.

CPSIA information can be obtained at www.ICGtesting.com
Printed in the USA
242642LV00001B/2/P